The

Over the Moon

The Cow Jumped
Over the Moon

The Strange and Extraordinary Tale of a
Nervous Breakdown

Rachael Malai Ali

ONEWORLD

OXFORD

THE COW JUMPED OVER THE MOON

A Oneworld Book

Published by Oneworld Publications 2007

Copyright © Rachael Ann Malai 2007

ISBN-13: 978–1–85168–458–8
ISBN-10: 1–85168–458–1

Typeset by Jayvee, Trivandrum, India
Cover design by youngs design
Printed and bound by TJ International Ltd, Padstow, Cornwall

Oneworld Publications
185 Banbury Road
Oxford OX2 7AR
England
www.oneworld-publications.com

This Book is dedicated to my nanna 'Norah Joan Campbell', to my five children – Azim, Dani, Qawi, Bazil and Marshya Rose – to my Mum, Wendy and my sisters Jenny and Paula . . . all who love me unconditionally. I love you too, with all the love in the world. And to Joel . . . whose arrival in my life could not have come at a better time.

Contents

Introduction

Hey diddle, diddle the cat and the fiddle,
The cow jumped over the moon.
The little dog laughed to see such fun
And the dish ran away with the spoon.

I have always felt an affinity with the cow that jumped over the moon: I can identify with her. It can't have been easy accomplishing something like that, but she did it. She set her sights on jumping over that big old moon and went for it. 'Sod this grass munching', she must have thought to herself, 'cooped up in this field and getting my udders yanked about, I hate it . . . it's not me. I'm outta here!' Groovy cow that.

A few years ago I was like that cow, not in the sense I was having my udders yanked (nor do I have udders, for that matter) but in deciding to 'jump over the moon', to take a leap of faith by making up my mind to overcome nervous depression and panic attacks.

At the time I felt it was a hopeless scenario. I was trapped and cooped up and my life was an endless succession of doing nothing, day in, day out: all I did was worry and tie myself up in knots of fear and panic.

My name is Rachael. I am 38 years old, and once upon a time I had a nervous breakdown. That's what it was called. A nervous breakdown: a breakdown of my nerves.

A nervous breakdown is not usually something that one likes to discuss; after all, it's embarrassing. You can't really go to a dinner party and have this little chat over the first course . . .

'Hi, I work in advertising. What do you do?'

'Hi . . . advertising? Ooh . . . that's sounds interesting! I'm a nervous breakdowner. Would you mind passing me the bread rolls? Nice weather we've been having don't you think?'

But seriously – and let's be adult and grown up about this – people never talk about things like that. We would rather remain quiet, pop a valium into our mouth and float through life on a cloud of anti-depressants.

I, however, *do* want to talk about it. I want people to know how terrible a nervous illness can be. I want them to understand that a nervous illness is most probably the worst kind of illness ever. Why? Because you can't see it and you can't tell people about it, and thus you suffer.

Perhaps you have opened this book because you want to know how to jump over the moon. Or maybe you or someone close to you is having a difficult experience dealing with anxiety, depression and panic attacks.

If it is you, then I hope my experience can be of some help to you. If you are trying to understand how someone close to you is feeling and just how strong they really are, then I pray you will be able to help them more. No matter how they appear to be, they are *still* the person that you know and love on the inside. Trust me.

Those of you who are dealing with nervous illness and a tired mind may feel that you can't concentrate long enough to focus on the words. That's OK. If you feel fidgety and agitated, just flick through the pages and read whatever you want to read. I'm sure you'll be able to identify with some of the feelings and emotions that I have written about: the things you can't fully describe but that scare you. I know all about those, so just take it slowly – there's no rush. I've written this for you and you can take all the time you need. All those feelings you go through are your body gearing up for 'fight or flight', but there is nothing there except your fear.

Sometimes it may seem that your whole day is spent in a cloud of anxiety and gloom and you don't know what to do. Do nothing. Allow those feelings to come – let them, but understand that they cannot harm you because they are just 'your feelings' from 'your mind' and the only power they have is the power you give them.

The other thing I want you to know is that you are not alone in feeling like this. I was convinced I was the only person in the entire universe who felt this way. I used to worry about going to the shops, about talking on the telephone; I used to worry about being worried! Perhaps you too, think nobody in the world feels as bad as you – nobody could possibly understand what you have, no words can describe just how terrible you feel. Well, try me.

Although we may have different symptoms, although we may have different worries and fears, I can honestly assure you that I know and understand how you are struggling. I know you cry and feel alone, I know you wonder when, if ever, this affliction will end, I know you are perhaps resigning yourself to the fact that you cannot get better and are not sure how much more you can take.

You want to feel better so badly, you've tried everything and as far as you're concerned nothing is working. Well, let's take it slowly. Understand that you are in a fragile state of mind. Don't place demands on yourself because they will work against you subconsciously. In the back of your mind you may be expecting immediate, foolproof cures and when they don't happen, you'll lose hope again. Don't pressure yourself at this stage – it won't work. And *don't* compare yourself to others, because what works for one person may have absolutely no effect on another. Be kind and forgiving to yourself.

Slowly means a second at a time. It means being gentle with yourself. Slowly wins the race. Slowly is perhaps the opposite of what you have been doing because you feel so highly strung and jittery. Do you feel under pressure to get better? Afraid you're beginning to annoy people? Family and friends think you should 'get your act together'? All this plays on your mind too – constant demands and your brave attempts to pretend you 'feel a bit better' when in fact you really don't.

People are concerned because they love you and care for you – it's just that at the moment you can't quite handle it. Well, that's fine, and even if they do get ratty and snappy with you, that's fine too. They can't understand what they are not experiencing. It's nobody's fault – not yours, not theirs. Don't try to over-explain yourself. If you see that they look confused or pull a face, leave it. After all, not everyone will understand. Focus on *your* needs first at this stage: it's not selfish, it's a necessary part of getting better.

As you go through a panic sensation understand that it will peak and subside. It will subside – it has nowhere to go, see? Go through it and don't hold back or struggle – that will simply tire you out and make you more exhausted. See it for what it is, a temporary feeling that does not deserve all the time you are giving it. Yes, I know that it is easier said than done. I know how difficult it is to fight your way through a panic attack convinced that something is about to happen to you. I know how awful the sensations are, but the more attention you pay to them the bigger and scarier they will seem, especially to your tired mind. So, little by little, try and breathe your way through, stay with each peak, focus and do not fight: it's the fighting part that wears you out. That's why you may tingle and tremble afterwards. It's like a head rush in your body. It's a body rush.

Now, let me ask you. After all that panic and tensing up, after all that running around, gasping and choking, after all that sweating and sighing . . . What happens? You felt like you were being suffocated and were about to die, you thought you were going to faint perhaps or be sick . . . you struggle and fight, you cry and feel uneasy . . . this lasts for around five or even ten minutes. On a bad day it happens over and over again . . . but then, after all that struggling and fear what happens? *Nothing!* Because nothing was ever going to happen.

You are merely reacting to strange physical sensations and, by struggling and getting anxious, you are causing them to get worse. Nothing is going to happen. Nothing was ever going to happen in the first place.

It takes a very courageous person to go through each day while trying to cope with anxiety and nervousness. You keep so much inside: you smile when you feel terrible, you try to stop your hands from shaking, you sit at home too scared to go out . . . you feel that there is no hope left and your life is going to be like this forever and yet you still carry on. There are people who depend on you: you are the breadwinner and you can't let others see you fall apart . . . You try selflessly to meet the demands of daily life while ignoring your own. You fail to see your worth and choose to ignore your needs until you begin to feel like you are driving on an empty tank. But you're not empty really. You're just in a different frame of mind and you can't seem to understand how to get out. Everything seems bleak and gloomy.

I am not a doctor or a psychologist, or an expert in the field of mental illness, but having experienced a nervous breakdown which manifested as panic attacks, anxiety and depression and after struggling with it for almost two years I wanted to tell others who may be going through something similar that it can and does get better.

Do not, however, force yourself to face them – that's not the idea, and it will make you feel just as tense. Simply understand that you are choosing to start getting better and that you know that you can, and even if it takes time, you know that every day you have a better understanding of this illness and are starting to see that it needs to move on because you don't want to play any more.

I have written this book as if I am talking to a friend that understands. And I know you will. I want you to see what I experienced; I want you to get to know me. Perhaps we are the same . . . Perhaps you will recognize some of the symptoms which I had. I hope you do, because it will show that those silly panic attacks are not that clever – they could at least be unique!

I have also included excerpts from the journals I kept; it was these journals that gradually helped me realize that although some days were worse than others, they usually had the same pattern. They illustrated my illness for me and were a map that helped me track down the place I had started from. My journals revealed a great deal to me. What I thought were just panic-stricken notes and wobbly diagrams were actually subconscious feelings that needed to come out. My diagrams were pretty good too. (Actually, I became very, very good at drawing!)

I cannot promise you a 'magic cure' and I know how much you want it, but what I can give you is assurance. Assurance that all those weird, awful, depressing feelings are merely your mind's way of showing you that something is 'not right'. All that darkness, all those 'bad days', the different sensations and fears . . . it's coming from you and, eventually, given time and patience you will realize this. You are not crazy, you are not weird or strange . . . you are not being 'punished'. What is happening is that your mind and body are trying to help you see that, perhaps deep within, you have been suppressing a lot of things and perhaps now is the time, if and when you are ready, to start looking at them. And you know, they may not be as bad as you feared.

Those who have never experienced anxiety and nervous illness – or tiredness as I prefer to call it – may think it a little strange, but stick with me and you'll get the picture.

Journal entry:

I am like this but it's not fate, it's merely a trial to
    aggravate.
Oh do not mock the people who
Do not behave the same as you
It is not fair, you cast them down.
You shout and laugh
They sigh and frown,
Do not ignore them
It is not right
But help them win their mental fight.

Chapter One

Miss Rachael in the dining room, with the coffee

Journal entry: It's like I have no sense of reasoning or logic . . . people don't really understand, they think it's silly.

It's a funny old world, isn't it? There you are, sitting eating a sandwich and drinking coffee, everything in place, nothing on your mind and suddenly – wham! You're overwhelmed by an ice-cold terror that appeared from nowhere. You try to scream for help but realize that nobody can hear you because the screams are coming from somewhere deep within you and sheer terror is keeping your mouth shut, making you swallow your fear again and again.

Or you can be in the supermarket reaching over to pick up a packet of soap powder, feeling fine . . . then you can't breathe properly and want to drop everything and run. You could be sitting twiddling your pencil in a meeting, eating a nice meal in a restaurant, daydreaming on the bus, doing the laundry, having a shower, chatting on the phone – ordinary, everyday things that can be destroyed in a second. The instant those feelings and horrible sensations wash over you, the ordinary world becomes a terrifying place and every breath you take feels like it will be your last. That's what happened to me, anyway. My first full-blown anxiety attack happened when I was sitting at the dining room table, with that sandwich and coffee. That's all I was doing. Not bothering anyone, not thinking about anything in particular – it just crept up on me. Literally. It arrived, like a withered, whispery evil stranger. Without warning. It was there and unraveling inside me . . . a very uneasy, strange feeling that I was unable to breathe.

The sensation came on rather slowly. I remember feeling a little 'smothered' and uncomfortable, that I was not able to get enough air. I was scared – actually petrified is more accurate. So I just sat there, hyperventilating and not knowing what the hell was going on. Gradually the feeling built up until I was close to struggling to breathe but I was too afraid to say anything – and what could I say? Anyway, there was no one around: I was alone. And trapped.

How to describe this feeling? Like being at the bottom of a swimming pool and struggling to make it to the surface? Like there was a balloon wrapped around my face? What? Words failed me, so I clutched the tablecloth and waited to die. The air seemed thin now and no matter how many deep breaths I took, I could not get enough oxygen. My chest was tight, as if it was too small to get enough air for me, and I kept rubbing it, desperate for air to get in. I moved around in my chair, shifting and gasping for air. My heart was pounding fast and my cold damp palms clung on to fistfuls of tablecloth. I could not hear anything except the blood thundering in my ears as I pitched my way through an adrenaline-zapped rollercoaster of emotions. It was torture.

The power of imagination knows no bounds, especially when coupled with an exhausted mind. 'Oh fuck!' I thought 'I'm dying.'

After an entire five minutes (maybe less) it went away and I was left none the wiser. Had I eaten something? Was it an allergy to coffee and tablecloths? Was it asthma? Where had it come from? Anyway, it had gone so it was nothing to worry about. I had been rather stressed, I guess, about things in general – work, family, life, world peace – and I was not sleeping well, but I carried on. It was nothing to worry about, life is like that. Actually, that's not entirely correct. I wasn't rather stressed, I was very stressed.

I used to be Rachael: that was me. I wrote scripts, composed songs and had appeared on both Malaysian and Brunei television. A bit of a star, then. I speak Malay fluently and that, I think, was my biggest selling point. An English girl who can act and sing and speaks Malay perfectly . . . a novelty act. Went to drama school, got my diploma a year early and the sky was the limit – and I love the sky, especially when it's all twinkly and shiny with glittery stars.

I was very, very groovy, and when I was thirteen and a bit my parents sent me to a public school in England where everyone said 'yah' instead of yes and the parents all owned manors and farms and were somewhat distantly related to Churchill. Plus, of course, one has to wear one's collars up and call most everyone 'daaling'. Fuck. I was up a creek without a paddle initially. I arrived with my tuckbox full of dried cuttlefish and other local Brunei snacks, some neatly labelled Marks and Sparks underwear, and not a single taffeta ball gown in my trunk.

I'd been brought up in Borneo for crying out loud! And what does 'yah' mean? Talk about culture shock. I remember my first night distinctly. A hard iron bed, a puffy new duvet and all these strange English girls yapping about cricket captains. It was awful. I needed the safety of my warm Brunei place, smelling my grandma's cooking and being able to run around in bare feet.

I went on to spend five years of my life at Lawnside, my school in Great Malvern, and they turned out to be the most creative time of my life. I learnt how to wear my collars up, say 'yah', go to balls and eat very, very small cucumber sandwiches. I learnt that I was quite clever and got lots of O and A levels, and was even made a prefect. In fact, I was pretty OK back then, and very together most of the time. Then my parents marriage broke down – and our wonderful spoilt lifestyle started to disintegrate right in front of my eyes.

I went on, however. I worked at the TV studios here in Brunei before moving to Kuala Lumpur and getting a chance to work with a top Malaysian director called Shuhaimi Baba, a little tyrant of a woman who taught me a great deal. The main thing I learnt from her was to carry on and to never take no for an answer. I guess she was a big influence on my life because I turned out to be a lot like her – tough in some ways but very soft in others.

OK, I'm rabbiting on, but I just wanted you to know a bit about me. I am trying to say that I was a creative, outgoing person . . . so that you can see what happened to me when I broke for a little while, and so that you can understand that *no one* is perfect and it's OK to be broken because you can get fixed. Sellotape and all. And I still say yah and call everyone daaling or sweetheart. Very pretentious.

Looking back now I see that I was a bloody mess of a woman.

I resembled a blob and spent the entire day dressed in a baggy t-shirt and ugly black leggings. I wore huge, granny knickers with holes in them and my bras were all beige, kind of flesh-colored boulder-holders with thick straps that dug into my flabby back. I had three stomachs and could no longer see my belly button, which was just a distant dimple among the bulges. And when I stood up my feet disappeared!

My bosoms dangled below my knees like overripe papayas and my thighs resembled jelly and would kind of wobble against each other when I walked. Not exactly sex on legs, alas. With my short, convict-style haircut, from a distance I could easily have been mistaken for the Michelin man – except that the Michelin man was probably more attractive.

Once upon a time, six years prior to my metamorphosis into a walking blob, I had been pretty attractive. I would stop myself in the streets with my good looks – that's how lovely I was. (OK, so I'm exaggerating, but I had really let myself go, without noticing or caring.)

Why is it that once we get married and start a family we tend to become plumper and neglect ourselves? Do they call it 'settling down' because we turn into settees? At that stage in my life you could have put me in a sitting room with some Chippendale furniture with a few chintzy cushions on my lap and somebody would have sat on me (and quite comfortably, too).

Not everyone does this, I am sure. I did though. I lost my identity, my 'Rachaelness'. I was very much in love with my then husband, who is a Bruneian, previously married with three children from his previous marriage whom I really did not get on with at first. Regardless of this, I adored him: he was the bees knees, the caterpillar's boots, the colors of a butterfly – and I was on a mission to prove that I was an excellent wife and mother, who could run the house, work, look after the children, cook and probably fly too! The problem was that I was heading underground – but then I've never been that good at directions.

So, that was it. I was married and lost. I had thrown all my needs out of the window, folded up my wings, put them in a suitcase, stuck an Ever-ready battery up my bottom and set off on a journey. Getting fatter by the day and more stressed out by the second.

But did I complain? Did I say 'Excuse me, need a break, feeling like a dog'? Of course not! Don't be silly! That would mean I was weak and selfish! That would *prove* I was incapable and not grown-up and clever. So I lived a lie – a lie that eventually overtook me and became my reality.

I don't know what happened to me. I guess I took the wrong path – but you know in many ways it could have been the right path, because in a funny sort of way it did lead me to enlightenment. The weakness made me stronger. ('Enlightenment' means being full of light as opposed to being full of dark . . . I think, in which case it would be 'Endarkenment' . . . just a theory.)

I was so worried about money that I would devise all kinds of inventions and scribble out business plans. I was so worried about my baby smothering or getting ill that I would sit staring at him asleep in his Moses basket while nudging him all night. Imagine every time you're about to nod off, being prodded to see if you're awake. How annoying that must have been for him! I was so worried if my husband came home late from work that I would sit on the back step staring at the cars, waiting for his to turn into the driveway, then, relieved that he was back, I would resume my 'I Am Normal' act as if nothing was wrong.

Worries kept me awake all night long. They would chatter in my head incessantly like rabid squirrels, or thump around and give me headaches. Like a monkey in the jungle, I would swing from one tree of worries to the next. Today's tree was worrying and tomorrow's looming threateningly on the horizon. Occasionally I would let a little worry slip out and then immediately cover up by pretending it was nothing serious. My husband never seemed worried, but this simply proved how pathetic I was. I had so much to be grateful for. 'Look around,' I would say to myself, 'starving children, wars, sickness, and all you do is worry and feel sorry for yourself!'

In this anxious state food was a great source of comfort and I began to binge my way through each day. Stodgy food was the best: it gives you a nice comforting feeling as it expands roll upon roll around your waistline . . . I could stuff down a whole packet of biscuits in ten minutes, wash it down with coffee, puff on a fag and then reach for another packet of biscuits. I reckoned that if I could not handle my worries I might as well eat my way through life. It became a series of quick, sweet fixes and cigarettes were also very helpful, as was coffee. Nothing like a cocktail of nicotine and caffeine to get you high. Driving the children around was like going on a mobile food-fest, stopping at the little Indian grocery and buying packets of sweets, chocolates, fizzy drinks and not even wanting to share them because I was such a pig.

I was definitely on the right track for a breakdown. Everything was going to hell and I didn't seem to be able to stop it – I didn't care enough to stop it, at this stage.

But I so loved being with my children. One thing about children, the beauty of them, is that they accept you for who you are, no matter how ugly you look, how frumpy, how grouchy. They love you unconditionally and there is no nicer, more magical, cozier feeling than getting sticky kisses and big hugs from a child. Being with my little men was a good feeling and no matter how bad a day was, the smell of their hair or the sound of them squabbling outside helped me to cling on to some semblance of normality – after all, I had to be there for them. If there was nothing else in my ugly world I had to keep on going for my babies.

Oh but it was awful, the depression, anxiety, worries. It was bloody, sodding awful. I felt like a faded old t-shirt that had been washed so many times it had turned a drab gray. There was no beginning and no end to the worries. I could not pinpoint any particular trigger, any specific event that had set them off, but they were with me constantly, fretting and tugging at my nerves and playing havoc with my brain. Still, I kept them all well hidden, stacked up and locked away inside. I was supposed to be a responsible adult after all – but in fact I was really 'the great pretender'.

I have never really grown up, I guess. I used to think that getting married, having children, a home, playing house and using a handbag and high heels was a guaranteed sign of being an adult – what I never

realized was how much bloody effort it took. Having children especially entails a lot of responsibility, and I never thought I was a good
enough mother.

I believed I had to be picture-perfect and when I found myself
unable to cope with the high standards which I had created for
myself I hated it. Honestly speaking, though, I am crap at being
responsible. I always wake up late, I forget appointments and I stumble my way through life. I am very messy and disorganized and I have
the utmost admiration for people who have diaries. Or those other
things – the little electronic things with pokey-looking sticks: personal digital diaries. I don't know how to use them, but I think that
people who use them are so clever – and damn trendy.

I am a bit of a slob and always leave wet towels on the bathroom
floor and, although I like washing up, I hate putting the plates and
cups away and prefer instead to build a high pile which I then cleverly
cover up with a tea towel. My handbag is a treasure trove of rubbish
and always seems to have bits of grit at the bottom and lipstick
which has melted (why?). I believe that mornings happen too early
and the official worldwide time for waking up should be just before
lunchtime at the earliest and that everyone should be allowed to go
to work in their pajamas.

There you have it. I don't know why God made me a mother to
five amazing little people when I am still very much a child myself.
On a bad day I reach for Enid Blyton and my teddy and have a good
thumb suck – it's therapeutic. But me? A responsible Mum?

Good Mothers have 'routines', they measure the milk formula
spoon by spoon rather than chuck it all in, shake the bottle and then
stick in their finger to taste it, and they certainly do not allow their
children to run around all day in their pajamas. Good Mothers always
look neat and tidy and have coffee mornings and compare notes. They
chop up bits of carrot and celery for their children's lunchboxes and

wrap up peanut butter sandwiches in cling film: they would never simply microwave a whole packet of hot dogs, chuck them into a bag and reheat them for dinner if the children don't finish them at school.

They sit and do homework with their little ones, patiently working out each little sum and pointing out 'Peter, Jane and Pat'© at the seaside. They certainly do not say 'Not more bloomin' homework!' or make derogatory comments about calling a dog 'Pat' or the fact that Peter and Jane's mother is unliberated and spends all of her time in an apron, tied to the kitchen sink in domestic bondage.

I wasn't a member of the Good Mother Club or a responsible, well adjusted grown-up. To be an efficient grown-up you have to make lists and pay bills and keep the fridge stocked up. You have to be up early to get the children to school and do the grocery shopping and stop for a chat when you bump into a fellow grown-up. You have to be able to have interesting conversations about mortgages and the economy, skin products that work for you and how your 'female down-below problem' is better with that new cream. You have to listen patiently and intently to others and say 'Oooh really?' with faked, wide-eyed interest when in fact you couldn't give a fuck. And of course you never say fuck. You say 'hoot'. Couldn't give a hoot.

A good grown-up would never admit to still sucking her thumb, having burping competitions with her sons and being afraid of the dark. This is me, a failure at 'grown-up dom'.

In my exhausted mind I was a complete and utter failure at everything – and I soon began to believe it and set myself on a self-destructive course without knowing know how to stop. It was happening all around me and I was out of control.

I survived on little sleep. It wasn't even sleep really, but tossing and turning, a sweaty uneasy lapse of darkness. My mind could not rest: nightmares were common and I began waking up at three a.m. In the early morning silence I would listen to my mind telling me about all the worries I had – all the problems, the ugliness, the doom and gloom, the bad things that were going to happen. It talked on and on and I, the unwilling victim, was being brainwashed by my own thoughts. I was in a horror movie and Alfred Hitchcock would make a cameo appearance any time now. (Actually thinking about it, I was beginning to resemble old Alfred. He was on the rotund side and had a few rolls of chin. Might as well look at things from an artistic perspective.)

However, I was still 'functioning'. I was managing to drag myself around by my fat little neck, I was able to muster up energy to move around like a robot. I considered myself to be worn-out and stressed and that was all – but surely PMT doesn't go on for months?

Anyway, as I was saying, on that particular day at the dining room table I experienced what I now know to be a 'panic attack'. I had, in effect, reached the peak of my despair, the summit of my mountain of worries, and was about to be thrown off into the unknown.

That evening my husband and I went to look at our new house and were chatting away in the car when suddenly the feeling came over me again. The shallow suffocating sensation and slow heavy wave of fear was there with me in the car and was so real that I froze in panic and sat staring straight ahead. Perhaps if I kept still it would not notice me. However, it worsened and eventually I began to whimper, then reaching for my husband's hand I gasped 'Can't breathe. Can't breathe.'

Not really a good thing to say to your husband when he is driving down a busy motorway. I vaguely remember him swerving to the side of the road and me clambering out of the car, gasping and struggling for air and thinking I was dying for the second time in a day.

It built up to a slow peak while I just waited, struggling to breathe and feeling helpless and terrified. This was death. This was me being attacked by a deathly invisible force. Somewhere in the background I could hear my husband asking if I was all right. Did I feel dizzy? But I couldn't answer him – it was too difficult.

Like labor pains, the feelings seemed to reach a very painful level, up and up and smother and smother and gasp and gasp . . . until finally they peaked and then subsided, and after a few minutes of standing hunched up encased in paranoia, I was able to stand up and breathe easier.

Whatever it was subsided and crawled back into the murky little pool from whence it came and I untangled myself, shaking, dizzy and wobbly: as my husband helped me back into the car, I could see that he looked pretty shaken up as well.

'OK? Feel better? Do you feel sick? Hot? What did you eat? You don't drink enough water! You need to drink water! How many times do I tell you? Water!' I should mention here that my husband's remedy for everything was water: headaches, tummy aches, back-aches? WATER!

Why is it that when you feel really shitty that you get yelled at for not taking care of yourself? I mean, you feel pretty rotten and then someone comes along and says 'I told you, you never listen.' There I was, helpless with fear and worry, being lectured on the benefits of drinking more water. I was too weak to argue and too worried to focus. The rest of the drive was a blur, the new house was a blur, I was a blur: on the way home my husband bought me a bottle of water and I took a few feeble sips to make him feel better at least. Once home I immediately made for the sanctity of my bed. Clambering in and pulling up the bedclothes around me I sat clutching myself around myself, my body uncertain of what would happen next. Had it really gone, whatever 'it' was? I was too scared to find out, I couldn't find out, and so I waited.

The room seemed gloomy and I was in homesick mode – that awful homesickness feeling that makes you feel sad and that something is amiss, that you need something to make you feel better: something familiar and safe? Whether it made sense or not – and how could I be homesick when I was at home? – that was what I felt, and I couldn't shake the feeling off. Something was wrong and I didn't know what – but it was out to get me and it would be back. It was a mental haunting, it wanted me and it would be back.

'Think cozy thoughts . . . think cozy thoughts . . . read a nice book . . . think nice happy things . . . smell your baby . . . hold him . . . relax . . . relax . . . relax . . . relax . . . sob . . . relax . . . sob . . . relax . . . But be careful . . . Aaaargh.'

It was no good. My imagination was working overtime and busily cooking up the worst-case scenarios. I was in the early stages of anxiety and far too fretful to be able to calm myself down. Of course, subconsciously I was waiting and wondering if it would happen again. It wasn't easy to forget such a smothering, suffocating, petrifying and morbid experience.

Yet I never assumed it was a serious thing. I thought I was being silly and should stop worrying and just get on with it. So I did. I got on with it. Everyone else was managing as far as I could see; everyone else seemed OK and was running their life. My friends, my family, my husband, my children, the people on TV, the people driving on the roads, the happy people of the world. Same world, different planet.

I was scared to relax and let myself go, because I had to be on the lookout, to be ready and alert. I felt vulnerable to an unseen force – as I was, in fact. It sounds self-dramatizing, I know, but it's how I felt.

Whatever 'it' was, had the power to reduce me to a nervous wreck and literally make me feel as if I was struggling to survive. I hoped it would not come back: perhaps I was over-tired and needed to sleep, to get some rest. I tried to reassure myself. I was scared. Very, very scared.

Chapter Two

Fight the good fight

Journal entry: If someone asked me to describe this 'affliction' I would say 'Imagine your worst fear and multiply it a million times . . . and that's only 1% of how awful this is . . . people with anxiety have a continuous background of noise to contend with . . .

After those first two incidents I was constantly on guard, but anxiously waiting for the next attack, and trying to put it out of my mind only served to make me more anxious. I was scared and did not know what to do. Who would help me? Would it be as awful as the last one? What if it comes when I am driving or in a shop? What if it happens when I am at work? All these 'what if's' formed a long queue in my head. I was obsessed with this problem, scared to over-exert myself in case I got breathless and the breathlessness would bring it back again – the monster waiting to attack.

Sure enough it always appeared. One afternoon I was at home and the awful suffocating feeling in my chest came over me, and my breathing felt shallow and I went cold. I tried to ignore it and walk around and sit down, stand up, put the TV on but it was there, inside me, suffocating me and trying to kill me. At least that's what my mind was telling me. Picking up the phone I called my grandmother who lived nearby and literally whispered that I could not breathe and to call a doctor now. Then I slammed down the phone and stood by the front door to wait for the cavalry to come and rescue me.

The cavalry took the form of my 78-year-old grandma, who arrived and made me sit down, then listened patiently as I tried to explain I was 'ill and suffocating'. She was very reassuring and said it was all right, and I could breathe, that I was breathing. Which kind of made sense – I *was* breathing. It felt like I wasn't but yes, OK I was. With difficulty but all the same, still breathing. Just about.

After it had peaked and slid to the back of my mind, I felt better. Usually after a peak I would feel light-headed and there would be a tingling sensation in my body. This became a comfort sign for me, a signal that it was over and I could relax for a while at least. Along the way I picked up many comfort signs and zones and positions, which I will talk about later.

It's not easy being a professional nervous breakdowner. Oh no. There is a popular belief that we are weak self-piteous wimps who are expected to survive on tranquilizers and shut up. Of course this assumption is usually given by 'experts' or people who never have experienced a nervous illness. And speaking of experts, why is nobody perturbed by the fact that Sigmund Freud, the so-called father of modern-day psychoanalysis, was obsessed by sex? The man related everything to it.

'Hello Mr. Freud, I keep feeling anxious.'

'Ya, vel zat would be a sexual psychosomatic symptom.'

'Hello Mr. Freud, I just can't seem to function.'

'Ahhh . . . vel of course . . . your sexual self is frustrated and rebelling.'

'Mr. Freud, would you fancy a bonk?'

'Ooh jah baby!!'

Plus, we don't actually break*down*. We *break*. The breaking-down process is actually just the preliminary stage – gradual and painful, it begins with little twangs of worry, little snaps of fear, little thuds of anxiety, and then develops into the 'coming to a stop' process, whereby we feel unable to function and focus, where everything is threatening and no one can make you budge, they push you and cajole you, they try to talk to you but you can't move from this depressive state of mind, and from there we progress into the 'fallen apart, broken into pieces' department where you have been pushed to extreme limits, feel like you are made of clay and have fallen off a cliff and into a deep well of despair.

Eventually you land with a thud, and the pieces of you are scattered for miles, but no one has seen you fall and you can't scream because it hurts too much. It's mind-numbing pain. This helplessness is when the panic sets in – the panic that you are doomed to remain broken and stuck for ever and ever. The panic that you are at the bottom of a dark lonely pit and don't know how to get out. You're trapped.

You know I must say I do love creative writing.

We remain stalwart to the end, us breakdowners: we never want to bother anyone, we choose to remain anonymous for as long as possible – it's embarrassing to let on that you feel weird and strange.

People just cannot accept it. They'd ask, 'Oh hello Rachael, how are you?' and I would be so very tempted to reply 'Well, you know my mind feels weird and I keep having bad thoughts and feeling strange and I want to run away but I can't cos I am scared and I can't sleep properly and I am really agitated all day long and I feel like I can't breathe, like I am suffocating and I am worried all the time and trembling.' Naturally their expression would change as they attempted to register what you are telling them, because well, really, it's not *quite* what they expected to hear and it's making them feel a tad uncomfortable, so they choose to dismiss it. And besides it's way too much information for the meat and poultry aisle of your local supermarket.

'Oh dear, poor thing. Try and get some rest. Bye,' they mutter politely before scurrying off casting furtive looks over their shoulder. So, you shuffle after them tugging at their clothes, your eyes in a glassy stare, muttering to yourself while dribbling at the mouth and snorting. OK, not quite, but that's what they're half expecting. Besides, I always used a handkerchief when I dribbled.

Knowing that most people would know what to say to me, I always answered 'Fine'. Fine was the safe answer. It's not within the norm to be mentally unwell, it's way out there in the 'Oh-oh, certified nutcase', league. It's not acceptable to admit to something that society does not really understand and would prefer not to engage with. Well, bum to society and it's silly little conservatisms – let's start listening to people with tired nerves and perhaps learning more. What differentiates a person with diabetes or toothache from a person with a nervous illness? Nothing. They're all human and suffering a pain.

Nervous illness can pick on anyone – it's not choosy. The most debilitating factor about anxiety and panic attacks is that you don't realize that you have them until they have more or less settled in, usually as the end product of a lot of stress and worry and tiredness that you have long been ignoring. You're not even aware of just how long it is. You assume that it's just you being strange, a bit stressed, when in fact your mind has become a fertile ground for nervous

thoughts to be sown and reaped. It cannot fight any more so the little seeds of worries and fears grow and grow until they take over your
mind, giant beanstalks of tangled thoughts all having a field day
('field day' – get it? Seeds).

The thing is, life goes on and we have to keep up with it, or at least
try. Us, the worriers of the world, the ones struggling with anxieties
and fears that weigh us down and cause us to cease to want to function. And oh, how we try. I swear we try. We *know* how people see us,
that we're perceived as weak and attention-seeking, but it's not easy
to keep up with life when you're having a hell of a time just trying to
keep up with your racing, agitated mind; when even getting dressed
and talking is an effort

And contrary to popular belief, we are not complete idiots either.
People who suffer from depression and other forms of nervous illness are in fact very intelligent, nice, and if I may say so, normal people – not cave dwelling in-bred fools. I speak for myself here of
course. But we are. This is what makes it all the more painful. We
know something is terribly wrong and yet it baffles us. I struggled to
rationalize my thoughts; I constantly attempted to overcome the
fears and the worries. I was acutely aware that not many people
would be able to fully understand my 'illness' and that if I remained
silent it would be easier to handle.

I abhorred being told to 'be strong', 'take it easy', and 'cheer up'
(damn people who tell you to cheer up!). I know it sounds ungrate-
ful, but 'don't worry, be happy' does not penetrate the wall of darkness that builds itself around this sort of illness. I wasn't a complete
whacko, and when people tried to undermine my illness and the very
real anguish which I was experiencing, I felt they were undermining
me as a person.

After all, what exactly does 'be strong' mean? Take up a crash
course in weightlifting? Flex your muscles? Lift up a bus with your

bare teeth while balancing a horse on your shoulders? What? Was I expected to swallow a tin of spinach and yodel 'I'm Popeye the sailor man'? Being strong had nothing to do with it as far as I was concerned – I had to be vigilant. Vigilant and alert!

And as for 'cheering up' – you're kidding me, right? I mean please, keep your little 'bumper sticker' advice to yourself before I slap you on the forehead, and the same goes for 'look on the bright side'. As opposed to what? The dark side? The dimly lit side? The dull side? And where was this so-called 'side' I was supposed to be looking at? Because the only side that I could see was the backside from which apparently all this nonsensical, empty advice was coming from and which I was sorely tempted to kick.

A nervous anxiety disorder does not diminish your intelligence. It merely hinders your ability to think properly and in an orderly manner. You're still the person with the nine O levels, a degree in horticulture and a Doctorate, you're still the microbiologist or the hairdresser with her own salon. You're still very much you, but in a different mode.

There are periods of clarity and relief, the days when you try to make sense of your pain, the days when you feel able to talk and to justify your odd behavior. It was during these quiet times that I would attempt to seek out my 'cures' or read articles. I learnt a lot, but nothing helped. Walnuts are very good for the brain, but no, eating one hundred at a time will not give you an immediate remedy. Neither will chewing on a whole bottle of zinc and vitamin B complex tablets. They are all just supplements to 'supplement' you – look, I read the *Psychiatry Today* magazine: I know what I'm talking about.

I gradually came to understand what Sylvia Plath meant when she wrote the lines 'Silence one would willingly devour it.' She must have had loud, noisy, ugly thoughts as well.

We try to keep up. We don't want sympathy and we do have pride. It's what I tried to do anyway. Keep up, carry on, stiff upper lip . . . But inside I was a wreck. How I cried and cried at night in the bathroom, huddled up on the floor and begging for the mental pain and yucky thoughts to stop! How I yearned to be all right and to not have to cope with fears and worries and prayed for them to evaporate away into thin air. After the first few attacks I told myself that it would not happen again. Little did I realize that by that time 'it' had moved in and was planning on staying for a long time . . . So much for being strong, cheering up and looking on the bright side.

Journal entry: I feel I am being deprived of the 'sense' to 'live' as all I do is exist with occasional spouts of being and feeling 'normal'. It is not apparent. I know my family think it's just a mood. But it's much deeper. Incredibly so. I have this awful feeling in my neck, like it's bruised inside . . . fell asleep only to be woken by a spasm in my left chest area . . . put me on guard. Got home after a hectic afternoon . . . feel like I can't get enough oxygen . . . like I'm about to pass out, like I'm dying. 'Oh Man, searchest thou not too far for faith, for faith lies within you awaiting to be woken . . .

A panic attack sufferer tries to create a logic as a coping mechanism and it is important that they have something to focus on to make them feel safe. However, sometimes they work so hard at distracting themselves that it can work against them. It gets very tiring trying not to think about the next attack, and the more you try to push them away, the worse they get.

After a few of these attacks I began to convince myself that I had a serious illness and that it was in my blood – possibly a stroke or my head or my heart. I began reading medical books to try and diagnose my ailment: my bedtime reading was a medical encyclopedia of symptoms and I would even take notes.

Eventually, of course, new symptoms arose. I started getting tight feelings in my chest or my breastbone area, spasms of pain would streak across and paralyze me into a robotic state. I would have to stand still and wait – like a big china cow.

Inside me the voice began. 'Do not move, keep still, watch out, it's coming again, oh God! What's going to happen . . . gotta get out . . . Need to find a safe place . . . Something is going to happen to you . . . no one knows . . . no one can see.' Afraid to move or walk or talk. Just wait. Don't do anything. You are about to die.

Journal entry: From 3.00 a.m onwards I was in a fitful agitated state . . . Went to work feeling on edge and generally awful, I mean, really awful. Have had that pain in my upper abdomen the whole day, very sore and painful.

My world became a very dark place. My mind constantly raced and thoughts would spin around in my head, all of them negative and gloomy. 'God is making you suffer before you die. You are trapped. There is no way out. No one can hear you' – but that's a very watered-down description of the actual feelings I had. All I knew was that I was constantly scared and in a state of anticipation that something bad was going to happen. I was on the defense. It was a battle of one mind and one body and I was somewhere in between, not safe in either one.

People have always seen me as being strong, obnoxious, loud and courageous. It was, I guess, a persona I invented to fit in. To find acceptance behind the charade. I became what people expected. I am good at that. Hey, I got a silver medal at the Cheltenham Arts Festival! I acted my way through life. There did not seem to be a niche for who I really was or am, so I joined the crowd.

My individuality did not, could not, fit in. I mean I was fuck at saving money and yet I was expected to look after a household, I was hopeless at waking up early yet I had children to get to school, I was bored by my life and I pretended I wasn't. I was angry with the way my marriage was so one-sided yet I convinced myself it was fine. Jeez, I screwed up.

As for religion. Well, with all due respect I found it difficult to pray because I knew (first-hand information) that God hated me anyway. I was desperate to find a way, to find peace, to be like the people I had read about who had difficult times and then suddenly everything falls into place. But it never happened to me.

My knickers had holes in them, my dress sense was borderline absurd and my thoughts were totally gaga. It was all I could do to hold myself in place. I did not dare speak up. Sure, I was loud but, whatever I *said* was never true or real to who I *was*. My life was on loan and I had to pay back with my reasoning and sanity. I did not know what I wanted, but I knew it wasn't what I had. I wanted to be happy and not to worry and yet all I did was bloody well worry. And it's so much easier to be sad than happy. Happy is for other people and being happy is stupid. People with problems are the ones who know what life is all about.

It's a pretend world we live in. Back in the Stone Age I am sure everything was much more honest. I for one would have been quite happy running around semi-naked covered in a bit of fur (fake of course). I would probably have dyed it fluorescent pink and spent most of my days carving poetry on cave walls. There wasn't much conversation back then except for an occasional grunt and I am sure everyone was much more together.

Basically we are all afraid. That's what my illness taught me. It taught me that I was afraid. I was afraid to face my feelings and to let on that I felt used, abused, tired, ugly, stupid and poor. It taught me that I was not being true to myself and that I needed to face certain feelings. The one big pain of that illness was perhaps the accumulation of all the small pains that I had hidden. It taught me that over the years I had conditioned myself to be well-behaved and polite, not to offend people and not to discuss my emotions openly. I had conditioned myself to be practically non-human.

Society does not really like people who are too honest. They're a novelty item, fun fair material. I suppose that's why reality shows are huge successes – because we can watch people doing things that we can identify with without crossing any boundaries of good behavior ourselves. The human race loves seeing people's vulnerabilities exposed. That sounds rude, but we do – and we laugh at them while secretly being painfully aware of our own.

I was only happy when I was sad – and I did not dare be too happy. My self-esteem was so low that sadness and worry became my constant companions: I denied myself the freedom to live and enjoy it. As far as I understood, life was basically not a happy thing. I wanted to be grazing lazily in a green meadow but that could not happen. I had to keep up. Walk that stupid walk and talk the stupid talk: then, and only then, will you be accepted.

But we are all still scared, and not many people can face up to their fears. It's much easier to ignore that little voice inside – I did until it decide to shout at me.

Journal entry: My hyperventilating started around mid-afternoon; it's so awful because it feels like suffocation from the inside. I was so scared but I didn't show it. Then I got agitated . . . I feel so lonely . . . fear is sitting in the back of my mind with his lips curled into a smug smile as he rocks in his chair . . . Still haven't figured out a way to kill him yet.

Chapter Three

All I want for Christmas is my sanity

Journal entry: I am being deprived of joy and hope.

The tree was up, so was the giant snowman that the boys and I had made. The shopping was not completely finished but then I have always been a last-minute shopper. Christmas was coming and in between the wrapping and the sticking, the buying of cranberry sauce and boxes of chocolates, the decking of halls and the jingle of bells, I wondered if Santa was going to give me some peace on earth – or was I on the naughty list?

I love Christmas! Everything about it makes me feel all fuzzy inside. My sisters, Jenny and Paula and I, were brought up to appreciate both Western and Eastern culture. This meant we had the best of both worlds. We celebrated Hari Raya, which is known as Eid, the celebration after the holy month of Ramadan which is the Muslim fasting month. In Brunei it is the most highly anticipated festival of the year. Colored lights decorate the houses, cakes and cookies are baked, women wear new, delicately embroidered *baju kurongs* (the traditional dress of Brunei, a long, A-line blouse with a tiny V-cut neckline on to which it was customary in the old days to pin a gold brooch). The skirt is long and flows past the ankles. These days the *baju kurong* has evolved into many fashionable designs and the women of Brunei are very particular about keeping up with what's new. They literally sparkle at Hari Raya with their beautiful beaded skirts and sequined blouses and dressmakers in Brunei do a roaring trade in the weeks before Hari Raya.

The men wear *cara melayu*, an outfit which is very similar to a smart pair of pajamas, and a *sinjang*, a short sarong, tied around the waist. The *sinjang* is hand-woven from gold and silver thread and has intricate flowing designs of flowers and Malay art embroidered on it. Now I sound like a travel guide. In a nutshell, everyone looks damn fine.

Anyway, it is a wonderful festival and I have continued the custom of celebrating both Hari Raya and Christmas with my own family. I'll do anything for a party. All was going very well that Christmas day, the turkey was wonderful, no lumps in the gravy, my roast pumpkin delicious and only the chocolates with the yummy centers eaten . . . it had been a lovely day, right up until the point where I was sitting unwrapping my Christmas presents. As I sat on the sofa clutching my half-opened present it came and no, it wasn't the Christmas Spirit. The room started to sway and it was difficult to breathe.

Everyone was talking and laughing, and Mum was looking at me expectantly, hoping I liked her gift. I couldn't see it. I couldn't see a damn thing. Everything was a blur. My hands were cold and my chest was tight. I felt sick and scared and needed to run. I had to run. I was vaguely aware that everyone was looking at me now – well, it was difficult not to notice me actually, sitting there puffing and wheezing and trembling with a mortified expression on my face. I looked like Mrs. Santa on heroin. Excusing myself I made a mad dash once again for the sanctity of my room, my 'safe place' where I sat on my bed and waited. I was suffocating at Christmas. Mum must have thought that I really hated her present.

Journal entry: It had not even allowed me to have Christmas. It was unpredictable and cruel. I was being haunted and tormented and there was no telling when it would rear up its ugly little head. I was not safe. This meant that I had to be prepared. There would be no warning.

At work one day, I remember demanding my Mum to take me to the hospital. At that time I had been doing some part-time teaching at my mother's kindergarten. I loved it; the children were aged between three and five and were great little people and we had a lot of fun. Being a big kid at heart, I loved nothing better than painting and water play, and often made more mess than my little colleagues.

However, it was becoming increasingly difficult being Aunty Rachael. The children's laughter and chattering frightened me and seemed loud and threatening. I was always on edge and no longer able to make toilet roll spaceships and fluffy rabbits. Singing and dancing was out of the question in case it brought on a 'spasm' and each day was an effort. As for sitting in the staff room during my coffee break – well, that was sheer hell.

Of course the other women could see that something was wrong with me but were too polite to say anything. I was after all, the boss's daughter. The one sitting in the corner with a strained expression on her face and a sign around her neck saying 'Sod off the whole damn lot of you. I bite!'

On that particular morning I had an awful spasm in my chest and immediately felt sick and began to tremble. I needed to get to the hospital. It was an emergency! Something was wrong with my heart. My head. My body. Sitting in the car, on the way to hospital. I listened to Mum talk as she tried to distract me. 'Ahaaa!' said the monster, 'nice try, but it won't work, *nothing* can take her attention away from me.'

Mum's voice kind of came and went in the gray thudding distance. I could hear it from behind a muffled wall, a thick carpet in my ears. I wanted to listen but I was very agitated. The car seemed to be going very slowly and I just needed to find a safe place. I was also trying to look as normal as possible. Looking normal is important. An anxiety sufferer does not like hassle. The well-meaning 'Are you feeling better? don't worry', only serves to agitate. Anxiety sufferers are not dumb, they are just not able to talk and focus at one time.

They need reassurance but it must be in tune with what they are feeling. By this I mean, if you ask someone at the peak of an attack if they are OK, you may not get a response. They may rush off, or cry and shake, they may cling to you, and they may look terrified – the best thing to do is to be there for them. Just be there for them.

Sometimes they appear rude and selfish, but they aren't, trust me. In fact they're doing their very best to maintain their dignity. What they experience during a panic attack is a whole range of emotions all crashing into their head and reverberating around their body. They're shaking and totally out of synch and desperate to regain control. It's not selfish. They try to be as selfless as possible – if only you knew. They are just trying to keep an outer calm on the inner frenzy. They seem abrupt but it's just the anxiety, no one can see what's happening and they don't want anyone to witness them fall apart. They try so hard to appear dignified. Well, I did. I failed miserably, but I tried.

Later on as I sat in the emergency unit a nurse, obviously thinking I was having an asthma attack, tried to put an oxygen mask on my face. No help at all. I wrestled with her, my face contorting into a grimace and my hands clawing at the mask. She was very determined to get that thing on me and I was equally determined that she would not. The mask made me feel suffocated – it was like a big plastic glove. I was becoming almost hysterical and very, very agitated. I won the match and yanking off the mask I snapped at her to get the doctor.

The panic inside me was surging and I felt the awful drowning sensation as it overtook all sense of time and space. Everything was wrong and I could not scream. My throat was rammed with a tight wad of fear. The nurse stared at me aghast as I jostled about on the white sheets, yelling for the doctor. To say that I seemed rude is probably an understatement – I was petrified and scared shitless.

Could she not see I was dying? That I was suffocating and that I was an urgent case? She was annoying me and aggravating me all at the same time because she did not understand my totally urgent predicament! I wanted to thump her. I wanted her to get a bloody move on! I needed to have tests done. Help me! Help me!

Mum told me to calm down, but by then everything was a black mass of terror and panic. My breathing was short and my chest tight, my eyes could not focus and I was morbidly petrified. It was like being stuck in a small room with no lights and no oxygen and footsteps were approaching. In the dark, something was coming. I wanted to run away but was too scared to leave. I wanted to be on my own but was afraid something would happen. The hospital seemed like the best bet. Everything was there if they needed to resuscitate me.

Eventually a doctor did arrive and I managed, in between sobs, to tell him my symptoms. To reassure me I was given an ECG and my blood pressure was taken. Everything was normal – but of course in my mind that was not true. How totally absurd! 'Normal?' Look at me for crying out loud! Do I look normal? There was of course some mistake. If it was not detectable on the ECG thingy then naturally it was my brain. It was inside my brain. I needed to be scanned! That was it! Get the scanner in here, get an ultrasound machine! Call the specialists! The doctor was wrong! Get another doctor – this one is stupid! I demand a second opinion! I was very ill, but perhaps it was not apparent on the machine. Perhaps the machine was broken? Perhaps the doctor was an incompetent nincompoop . . . the nurse certainly was. Where was the nurse anyhow? I hadn't finished with her yet either.

By now everything was mad, I was buzzing and shaking and unreachable. I was going through a tunnel of glue, it was in my throat, up my nose, and I was gagging on fear. People were clamoring all around me, trying to calm me down but it was pointless. I was agitated and scared all at once. Sweating and yet cold, breathless, blurry, wanting to vomit, wanting to faint, wanting answers, wanting to be saved. If the hospital could find nothing wrong with me then what was going to happen? How would they stop me from suffocating? How could they save me? Everyone was talking at me, rubbing my shoulders, cocking their heads to one side and saying nice, meaningless things. Being touched irritated me at that point and I would shrug them off. The nice yet obviously under-qualified doctor, my Mum, a friend who had come over to say hi, the nurse who was dithering in the background . . . all trying to help me. I couldn't handle it.

Here I was in the emergency room, tense as a scared cat, nostrils flared and once again hands clenched into tight fists . . . my breathing was erratic and felt labored, my thoughts were piercing and screaming 'Die! die! You can't breathe! No-one can help you!' With tears welling up in my eyes, I waited for death or something much worse to come and get me.

It's strange that when you feel scared you need to be reassured, but because you feel agitated and short-tempered you snap at those people trying to reassure you. They get fed up and angry at you and you are then left alone and, while you are very much aware of the dirty looks and scathing comments of 'being silly . . . perfectly all right really', you are unable to communicate, to voice your fears in a logical, eloquent manner. Plus, you're *still* trying to cope with the anxiety and fear, and you are *still* in need of reassurance, but nobody wants to reassure a quivering, rude, fat cow who has a tendency to hurl obscenities at them. Well, would you?

Agitation is a symptom; it's not something that we want to feel but heck, it comes along anyway. It's a panic attack package deal for one. A one-way ticket to despair. I lost count of the number of people I offended during a panic attack. I didn't mean to: if anything I needed that comforting and above all their tolerance, but inevitably I would snap and shake before skulking off into a dark corner to lick my wounded soul.

After the doctor had concluded that I was OK physically and as I was seemingly starting to calm down – i.e. had stopped chewing on the bedsheets and gnashing my teeth at the nurse – he suggested that he would make an appointment for me to see the hospital psychiatrist.

Psychiatrist? Did he say psychiatrist? Ahhhh . . . alrighty. That sounded quite serious really. 'Psychiatrist.' Well, I don't think so thank you very much Dr. Doolittle. Nope, no way, no how, not in a million years. Not a good idea . . . I wasn't going. Look, shouldn't you be doing more tests?

I was doing my best to appear composed at this stage, picking bits of torn bedsheet from between my teeth. How on earth was I going to get out of this? What was I to do or say? 'Look, I know I may have been a mite rude but do you think it could possibly have anything to do with this knee injury I had at school?' Or 'Is it perhaps food poisoning? Heat stroke? Could we discuss this doctor? What time do you get off work? We could grab a bite to eat . . . No, you silly thing,

I won't eat *you*. Ha, ha, ha . . . *see*, we're bonding. Has anybody ever told you that white is definitely your color? Well, it is. Very much so. Anyways, let's just forget I was even here shall we? Hey, what's a little bit of insanity among friends?'

No, I didn't know what to say and I was starting to get angry and irritable and uncomfortable again. Just because they couldn't find out what was wrong with me, just because my symptoms evaded them, just because I had some rare tropical illness which they had quite obviously overlooked I was being carted off to see some shrink? Hah! How pathetic was that? How did being a little bit breathless, getting a little bit snappy and perhaps ever so slightly panic-stricken qualify me for a psychiatric analysis?

Jeez, so I was a bit tired . . . what happened to freedom of expression? A person can't get over-tired any more? Is that what I was being told? Was it my fault that the doctor had not chosen to give me a brain scan, to call a neurologist, gynecologist or zoologist to render me a second opinion? Look, OK, fine, give me a few Panadol® and I am out of here. I am sure the psychiatrist is a very busy bunny and I too have places to go and people to meet. Defensive? Who? Me? No, I am not getting defensive! Oh! Riiiight! So I am getting defensive now? Is that what you're saying? Speaking my mind is defensive? So am I just supposed to shut up and be dragged off to see some psychiatrist?

Psychiatrists are for other people, not me! I'm not mental! I want to go home! I refuse to see a psychiatrist! It's my body that's ill and I notice nobody is going out of their way to do the necessary tests, very shoddy behavior on the medical profession's part if I may say so. The Surgeon General will have a lot to say about this I'm sure. You'll be sorry, oh yes indeed. Is anybody listening?

It was no use – nobody was listening except me. And finally it struck me that as I ranted on I was proving myself a suitable candidate for a psychiatric analysis. The doctor and my Mum had made up their minds anyway. I had no mind to make up at that point and had reluctantly decided that I did not care who I saw as long as they would make me better. I wanted 'better'. I was still very fidgety and scared, and being told you need to see a psychiatrist is not exactly good news, but better is what we're aiming for here.

The doctor went off to make an immediate appointment with the psychiatrist; in fact I'm pretty sure he was running. The nurse left me alone (to foam at the mouth and howl, no doubt).

Journal entry: Where are you my Creator?
Do not forsake me now
Invisible Narrator in whose story I do plough,
I'm reaping bitter berries, seeds I planted long ago
Their juice is black and sour, like something that I know.
It's a meagre, cruel, scorning drinking my own misery,
Oh dearest my Creator, throw down some faith to me.
(Can even be sung to a hip hop beat, or rap possibly ...)

Chapter Four

'Tell me about your childhood . . .'

Journal entry: I hate jolting awake . . . I want it to stop.
Every day people are wringing their hands in despair and
pulling out their hair trying to cure an 'illness' that can't be
seen. Its like walking up a mountain at night, blindfolded
with wild beasts around you.

   Mum and I sat in the waiting room of the psychiatric unit, which
was sparsely decorated with government furniture, a TV set, posters
outlining symptoms of mental illness and a lot of handicrafts obviously made by the patients. They consisted mainly of birds con-
structed from some kind of plastic card. At least I wasn't the only
one who wanted to fly away.

   My name was called and we were ushered into a small dimly lit room
where a kindly looking Indian man was seated. I scanned the room for
the proverbial couch. No couch. No straitjackets hanging on the

door, no electric shock equipment. Just three chairs and a bookshelf, desk, ugly carpet. The psychiatrist smiled, and introduced himself as Mr. Jadish (the name has been changed because I don't know how to spell it properly) and it began. The question and answer session. Would it start with 'Tell me about your childhood?' I wondered.

It didn't.

What seems to be the problem? How long have you been feeling like this? By that time I was feeling more lucid and was able to give intelligent answers which made me wonder if that was a good thing. Would he think I was wasting his time? That I was pretending? He asked a lot of questions which as far as I could see did not relate to my 'illness' – How was work? How many children did I have? What did my husband do?

How was this going to help me? All these questions! Yes, and I love salmon mousse and in my spare time I enjoy gardening and writing songs. Give me the cure *now*! (Agitation is a very large part of panic attacks.)

You gotta love psychiatrists though. They sit there, virtually expressionless, not giving anything away. They've heard it all before, I suppose. They don't frown, or laugh or shake their heads in despair. They don't make sarcastic comments or snigger into their handkerchiefs. They just sit there occasionally jotting a little sentence down, but not so as to distract you. 'I see', they'll say when you say you feel strange and fuzzy. 'I understand' they'll continue, nodding in all seriousness when you add that your brain is all muddled and noisy. 'Right', they'll carry on when you casually mention that you actually flew there in your supersonic spaceship which is parked outside on a double yellow line, and you have to be quick because you don't want to get a parking ticket plus you have to go save the world and the traffic at this time is just dreadful. Look you have to check to see if they're listening. They are.

You can say virtually anything in the world to a psychiatrist and they will accept it. Walk in dressed as John Travolta and start singing and you'll get no more than an 'I see'. Yes, they are true professionals. Psychiatrists. Beautiful people all of them. I love you, psychiatrists.

So there I sat, answering his questions as best as I could. I tried my best to show him that everything was fine at home but my Mum insisted on adding her two cents' worth — mothers. 'She has been a little bit stressed Doctor . . . home life.'

'Yes, but that's not it,' I growled from between clenched teeth.

'And a bit financial,' she added knowingly, with a little nod of her head

'Yes but it's not that!' I snarled in a loud whisper, obviously starting to look somewhat deranged and rolling my eyes up to the heavens at that ludicrous statement. I gave her a dirty look and started preening my fur for fleas.

'You see Doctor she keeps it all inside,' said Mum (without looking at me because I was staring daggers at her by then and she knew it). ('Strained relationship with the maternal figure', I envisaged him writing down.) Mum kept calling him Doctor. Everyone knows that psychiatrists are called Mister. Even I, the surly looking cow who was sitting staring at the psychiatrist's hush puppies knew that!

I was getting irritated again. It was not my home life, my finances, my anything — it was my head. I was ill; I was having breathing problems . . . it was obviously a physical sickness. I was in the wrong place. Mum was calling the guy Doctor and he was Mister, the room smelt funny and I needed to go to the loo. Everything was becoming fast and blurry again. It was all a mistake. Thank you very much Magnus Magnusson, it's been nice being interrogated by you, gotta dash, catch you later.

All these stupid questions seemed pointless and irrelevant and besides, there wasn't even a couch! Proper psychiatrists have couches. And wasn't I supposed to be hypnotized at some point? Not even a whiff of a pendulum. By that time Mum was answering most of his questions anyhow. I should have just got up and left them to it. Anyway, he made an appointment for me to come back in a fortnight and I was prescribed anti-anxiety medication, which I was later to discover were actually antidepressants.

Visit over, I walked out feeling like nothing had been solved and nothing was nothing. Everything was starting to feel like nothing. I was starting to sink into a far away place where no one could reach me and I was scared to come out anyway. I felt like a walking loaf of wet bread – heavy, sodden and bland.

What on earth was happening to me? And why me? Was there no one else on God's 'people to mentally torture' list? Was I so bad? Did this have anything to do with me yelling at Rosie Porter when I was at school and making her face go bright red? Or perhaps it was because I used to lie about my homework? Surely it wasn't the éclair incident? What sins had I committed that were causing me to be punished by my Creator? Having been brought up from the age of five in Borneo, a culture that prays five times a day and where everything revolves around religion and superstition and one that depends more on prayer and faith than on modern beliefs, it was inevitable that I looked to God for answers.

I had an idyllic childhood, full of sunshine and love. At the age of five I left behind 65, Foley Road, Birmingham 8, England where I had been living with my Mum, Nanna and Poppa. Mum was divorced from my real father, an Irishman from Sligo who had nice hands and loved poetry and classical music – and that's all I know about him. She had remarried to my stepdad, a Bruneian, so one fine day we boarded a plane and set off for Brunei, Borneo.

A place far removed from my little world of Rupert Bear and Mumfie the elephant, of roast dinners and Jaffa cakes, of Twinkle annuals at Christmas and where I could watch a bit of Coronation Street before going to bed at seven. The world I was about to enter was one of jungles and bare feet, mosques and festivals, where every day was sunny and mosquitoes would sing you to sleep at night before being gobbled up by geckos. I was excited but at the same time the prospect of leaving behind my darling Nanna and Poppa who had helped bring me up was inconceivable. It was a big wrench for a little five-year-old to deal with. They have always been the most special people and played a major part throughout my life.

I spent a lot of time at my Malay grandma Nini Bini's house, a big, bright wooden building five minutes from the South China sea. Nini could not speak a word of English and babbled on at me in Malay: small wonder that I soon picked up the language and within six months of arriving could gabble on like a real native Bruneian – the English Mowgli of the Borneo rainforests. Nini would take me to the market to buy coconuts for curries, fish and vegetables. All bartered down to an acceptable price and she would tell everyone with great pride that I was her 'chuchu', granddaughter from 'Englan'. Afternoons would be spent playing barefoot in the gardens of the grand old mosque next door and sipping hot sweet tea with the Imams who would be gossiping about 'old so and so' who never turned up for Friday prayers.

At night, after we had been bathed and smothered in talcum powder and Vick's, my cousin Jofrey and I would make our way to the neighbor's house. The neighbor had a new black and white television and it was the talk of the town. Dressed in pajamas and holding a little pillow (to sit on when we got there) off we would go to watch *Ultra Man*, a Japanese action man series. Every night we would arrive on their doorstep to watch telly. I'm sure that at some point we must have outstayed our welcome but this was a small matter to a couple of five-year-olds. We always made ourselves at home.

Every Friday would be house cleaning. All my aunties and uncles had their chores to do. Pillows and mattresses would be placed outside in the sun, sheets stripped and hand-washed in big tin basins, floors brushed, windows polished. My allocated job was washing the water bottles. In Brunei, water cannot be drunk straight from the tap so it is boiled and poured into bottles and then refrigerated. Nini would ask me to wash out empty orange cordial or Ribena^(tm) bottles, and I would sit on a little stool in the huge outdoor kitchen with the bottles all lined up full of soapy water and then with my special long brush in hand I would work up a real lather, thrusting and brushing them like there was no tomorrow, then rinsing them until they sparkled and were squeaky clean. It was a most enjoyable chore for a little British child.

Nini Laki, my grandpa, would have his big old radio blaring and would stand sipping hot black coffee while Nini Bini gave us our orders. Also, on Friday breakfast would be special. Roti canai, big fluffy Indian pancakes made from ghee and flour . . . all of us would pile around the long wooden table and Nini Bini would scoop ladles of thick, steaming hot curry over our rotis and pour out tall glasses of hot, sweet, black, local coffee.

Throughout the week there would always be some kind of celebration going on. Bruneians love celebrations and see it as a time for families to get together and eat and thank Allah for his blessings. Thursday night was Koran reading lessons. My cousins, aunties and I would sit quietly in front of the wizened little Imam, dressed in a crisp white shirt and a sarong, glasses perched on the end of his nose and a thin little cane in his hand pointing out what appeared to be squiggles to me. I was just about able to read Enid Blyton and understand the English alphabet – how on earth was I going to learn the Arabic one? Many a time I was rapped on the knuckles for not paying attention and being lazy. To this day I still have not fully mastered Jawi.

The big house was always full of people, aunties, uncles, cousins, great aunts, great uncles – my senses would be abuzz with sights, sounds and delightful smells. The big, dented stainless steel coffee pot brewing and steaming on the stove, Nini Bini standing grating coconuts, chopping onions and chillies while shooing chickens, kittens and stray grandchildren. Nini Laki in a sarong, listening to his faithful radio, the mosque next door calling people to pray five times a day. Yet somewhere between these wonderful experiences, surrounded by love and laughter, the day would come when I would have to grow up and leave a little barefoot girl behind. A little girl who ate rice with her hand, a little girl whose native tongue was Malay, a little girl who would fall asleep at night fanned by a sea breeze and be woken by her grandparents performing their prayers at sunrise. A little girl who always felt safe . . .

There are many days I wish I could rewind my life and stay in that childhood I was blessed with, but perhaps a lot of us do.

Prayer was, and still is an integral part of Brunei life and Islam is the main religion. Allah the creator is constantly worshiped and life in Brunei is centered around thanksgiving ceremonies, prayers, blessings and daily worship. In Brunei until recently mental illness within a family was usually kept quiet, because it was perceived as embarrassing and not something one wants other people to know. Mental worry or nervous illness is defined as *Uri* in Malay. Literally translated it means 'unreasonable fears'. In Malay culture there is a tendency to still rely on traditional medicines and the recitation of Koranic verses as treatment. That's not to say that a nervous illness is not taken seriously or is ignored, but there is still the lingering belief that a person may be in some way 'possessed'. Families prefer to quietly seek out treatment from wise men or religious teachers rather than risk the embarrassment of having a relative being admitted for psychiatric treatment and being talked about or shunned by such a small society.

Bruneians are very protective about their families and want only to do what they feel and believe to be right, both for their loved one and in the eyes of Allah. It is their culture and their way of life, and I respect that. Still, in all honesty it did cause a lot of arguments between my ex-husband and myself. You see, although I have been brought up in Brunei and I can speak Malay fluently, I was and still am fundamentally Western in outlook. Having been educated from the age of thirteen at public school in England, and only really moving back to Brunei when I was twenty-two, it was a clash of cultures, I suppose.

My ex-husband, however, had lived in Brunei all his life and comes from a very religious family who also believe in traditional medicines and so on – so one of my greatest hurdles was trying to convince him that I was ill and not possessed or mad. He does not really speak English, so I had to explain all of this in Malay, which was not easy because there were literally no words to describe my feelings! Apart from *Uri* I had nothing else to work with. It was like trying to build a bridge on unstable foundations. How could I make him understand me? I was having enough trouble trying to understand myself without having to translate it into Malay.

And it did sound silly and odd. 'I feel breathless, cannot breathe, am scared and need to run away' translated into Malay would simply be 'I got the *Uri*'s.' More often than not though I kept it to myself. I decided that it would just create more arguments if I were to try and explain, and I didn't need the additional hassle.

Eventually though, my husband thankfully began to realize and to see first hand that there is much more to a nervous illness than he ever really knew. In fact I don't think he ever knew that there are various categories of nervous and mental disorders. And, perhaps like many in Eastern cultures, he automatically presumed that you are either normal or possessed: there is no middle ground. In a way, though, a mentally ill person does appear to be possessed – our behavior at times defies explanation and yes, perhaps we do seem to be weird or crazy and it cannot be at all pleasant for our family or friends. Perhaps that is what upset my husband – I was behaving in a way that he could not comprehend.

I won't pretend it was an easy time for us – it was bloody difficult – but I am thankful that today we are still friends and he now at least understands and is sympathetic towards those that are experiencing any form of nervous illness. In fact, he often used to tell me about friends that he thought were having panic attacks or needed medical counseling.

I hate to think of the generations of people in this world who have suffered mental illnesses and been cut off from society. The pain and the sheer despair of not being allowed treatment and of simply being locked away. Even in Western cultures until the beginning of the twentieth century mental illnesses were treated with disdain and patients were subjected to horrible 'treatments' and experimented upon. I cannot imagine what they must have gone through.

I do believe though that God created us all to help each other, and in the Koran there is a chapter that says 'for every illness there has been sent a cure'. Sometimes prayer is not enough. One needs to have perseverance. That's part of the cure.

In an attempt to find my 'cure' I went to the two bookshops in the capital. Living in Brunei, there was no information to hand about nervous illness. In fact, there was nothing at all in Brunei about mental illness or anxiety. Apart from the local hospitals there are no other places where a person can seek help, there are no counseling or support groups. In short, I was on my own.

I managed to find one book entitled *Women and Madness* but it wasn't very cheerful reading, and I don't think it was intended for my category of madness. The author himself didn't sound very sane either and from what I gathered, had I been living during the Victorian era, I would most probably have been institutionalized.

I did come across another book whose title seemed to scream from the cover in bold print '*If you think you have a nervous disorder!*' and was illustrated with the cartoon of a rather insane-looking man whose hair was standing on end. This book thoughtfully listed the various 'life-threatening health problems that may arise from a stress-related disorder' – just the kind of thing you want to curl up with in the middle of a panic attack.

Then there was the 'natural way' to be free of anxiety and depression, but it involved a lot of reading and questionnaires which my tired brain could not digest. Everyone sounded like a know it all as far as my agitated, impatient self was concerned. Judging from their photos on the back covers all the authors looked happy and in control of their lives and had 'years of training and experience' dealing with people like me, but how pinpointing where my 'solar plexus' was could make a difference to my mental well-being had me stumped. I feebly attempted to open up my chakras and to picture myself surrounded by light, but perhaps I just wasn't ready to enter this spiritual abode of healing.

I also came across a book in which the author himself had suffered depression, but from what I read I concluded that he wasn't much better – the poor bugger sounded damn miserable, actually.

All I wanted was an easy, understandable, nice, friendly little book. Preferably a book with edible pages that would say 'Hello, do you feel like shit in a hot tin brain? I know how you feel and it's all right, yes it is, yes it will go away. Now if you just chew on page 8, entitled "instant cure for all the fears in the world" you will immediately start to feel better and you can then proceed to nibble on the corner of page 9.'

Mind: 'The organized conscious and unconscious mental processes of an organism that result in reasoning, thinking perceiving.'

Out of one's mind: Insane?

Insane: suffering from a mental illness.

Mental: Relating to the mind or its activity.

Question: If mental illness affects our intellect then why is it our spirit that takes such a bashing? It's enough to make anyone go mad really just thinking about it.

Journal entry: I am holding a lot of tension in my back. I am really quite a Loony bin.

Chapter Five

Dr. Rachael

Journal entry: I feel scared, angry and faithless. At times I want to run away from my body. Blood pressure 120/70. Cholesterol: 4.7.

I began writing my feelings down in a little exercise book. It was my 'mad cow journal'. My dad always used to call me a silly cow and now I was beginning to resemble one. The good thing about keeping a journal was that I could see how 'bad' a 'bad day' was in comparison to other days. I even created a 'demograph of emotions' which was a chart showing how much fear, faith, hope, happiness and worry I had. Fear, worry and anxiety were in the lead most of the time. Then I had my own terms, a language to describe the various feelings and pains. 'Soreioitis' for sore, 'twangisms' for the muscle spasms, the 'claw' or 'pickled-onion holder' for the gastric acidic reflux. At least I was being creative about the situation.

I also became very adept at drawing diagrams of the various parts of my body where pains occurred. There was my 'gammy leg' picture describing my thrombosis and/or rheumatoid arthritis as well as my bosom pictures (not that I make it a habit of sketching my bosoms but it was illustrative of the pains I felt around my breastbone area). Though this was perhaps madness, there was definitely method in it.

I would recommend keeping a journal to anyone who feels up to it. It was my pain I was reading about and I left no stone unturned. I would write everything down, word for word how I was experiencing it. If I felt like I was about to die I wrote that down, if I felt breathless and weird I would scratch painful sentences onto the pages. I wanted the thoughts out and this was the easiest way to do it. A lot of the thoughts were weird and strange. I didn't give a shit. How else was I going to release them?

The journal was one way of getting everything out of my system. Some days I could barely write, my hand would be shaking so much. Scrawl after terrified scrawl would line the pages – sometimes with diagrams and poems. I would draw witches and sad faces and would write deep, dark melancholic verses . . . anything to release some of the darkness and to let in some light. I would draw pictures of where my pains were. The tight, achey pains that made me shrivel up in fear and that would force me to look for a safe place. My body was constantly rigid as I was afraid to relax in case it brought on weird spasms. I needed to create safe places, safe body positions, and I could not handle standing up straight. I had to cower; I had to hunch up, preferably over the back of a chair or on my balcony. Anything that would stop my muscles from 'twinging and twanging'. I needed to be supported because I could not support my body. It hurt too much. Dante had nothing on me and I could begin to understand why Van Gogh had decided to chop off his ear. But I liked my ears and they were staying put.

Journal entry: Sometimes I get a 'Normal day'. These are good but make me suspicious. I think 'Hey, I have been OK, oh no ... That means it's going to come. I actually don't feel trustworthy of 'normal'. Normal is a lie. I have gotten so used to feeling abnormal. I feel the path I have been given is strewn with obstacles of my own making. I feel pressured and so alone. I feel sorry for myself ... I want to curl up in a ball.

One thing about giving medication to a person with a nervous illness is that sometimes they are scared of it. Perhaps I do not speak for the majority, but the minority out there who have ever had nervous illnesses or panic attacks are reluctant to aggravate the symptoms. Oh look, I was chicken, OK? Yes, chicken. See, I had a very big book about prescription pills and their side-effects. Every medication in the universe was listed, with glorious technicolor photos of the pills in question. It was great! The ones I had been prescribed sounded very nasty indeed. Side-effects included 'palpitations, cold sweats, nausea, and breathlessness'. Needless to say, this confused me because the side-effects were the very symptoms that I was experiencing. It was a Catch 22 situation . . . does the chicken come first or the egg?

There was only one way to handle this. I shoved my packets of pills in the back of my bedside drawer and ignored them. I was having a bad enough time coping with cold sweats and breathlessness as it was without having to deal with bloody side-effects. The psychiatrist was nuts to ask me to even contemplate undertaking such a gargantuan task. It would surely not be beneficial to my mental well-being. It was a bad idea and I was sure I would be able to manage. So stick that up your bum I said to myself as I slammed the drawer shut.

Things were not getting any better. I was obsessed with my body pains and any feelings I experienced would send me running to get out my medical encyclopedia. I would go to Mum's house and rummage through her little library for any medical or health books I could find; my grandma had a reliable old medical book from the thirties and I nabbed that too.

I had an insatiable desire to find reasons and cures. To see something in print that I could identify with. I even got out my son's picture book – *Your Body*, it was called, and had some very good illustrations of the tummy. I wanted to know specifically where my ulcer was and possibly my fibroids, hernia and liver spots.

I would read all the agony aunt columns in magazines trying to find if there were other people who were going through what I was experiencing and what was Dear Denise's advice? Usually though, Dear Denise would advise counseling or give a number for a local support group. Dear old Denise . . . And what the fuck does one do if there are none? (Only not fuck, hoot. Sorry.)

Journal entry: Have just been to the Dr's again with my acid reflux. Have had it since lunchtime and it is awful . . . Like I have swallowed bleach. Dr. Mui is very nice but I bet he must think I am a bit of a nutcase as I try to explain my symptoms, my words race out and my hands flap everywhere.

He prescribed some anti-acid meds and also something to calm me down . . . Xanax?\?????. A pretty little pink tablet. As I was leaving I remember apologizing for wasting his time, and he said 'Not at all, just to give you some reassurance.' Those words were like a hug: reassurance is a key part of an anxiety sufferer's comfort. We need reassurance: just something to make us feel a bit better because we are so frightened and our body and our mind do not feel as one. We do not want to hear 'snap out of it, pull yourself together, deal with it, you're so weak'. It's not helpful.

People with tired nerves and anxiety are not weak at all – they are very, very strong. A lot of the time they suffer in silence because they feel embarrassed or think that no one will understand what they are experiencing. They feel they may lose friends and support or be labeled as nuts. They fumble for words and try to make people understand, but if they get strange looks or sarcastic comments they will close up. They don't want judgmental remarks, and are intelligent enough to distinguish between genuine compassion and insincerity. Just because you can't see it, it doesn't mean that they're not feeling it.

At home I looked at the pretty little pink tablet and read up on its side-effects. It was just a mild relaxant and the side-effects were not too severe. I nibbled a bit off one before doing my squirrel routine and stuffing them in my bedroom drawer. The antacids my grandma could use: she liked to chew on gelusils®. Then I fell asleep on all fours. Who was I?

Journal entry: The main aspect about any kind of 'nervous illness' is that your brain, the one thing you depend on to function 'normally' has broken down. It has turned against you. It is not your brain anymore. It lives in your head but it is your enemy. Instead of helping you to focus and to think in a structured manner it LIES to you. So, where do you turn when your brain malfunctions? It's a cruel trick.

See, I did have some logical moments.

Journal entry: Witch in my brain. get out. be gone. Find some other to spook, be gone, and be gone! My mind is so out of it, anything can fool me now. People don't really understand, they think it's silly. Had an awful muscular spasm under my left bosom.

The worst thing is you have to pretend you're OK. You can be sitting there with all these weird sensations, pains, numbness, anxiety, fear, palpitations going on and yet from the outside you look fine. No one would even guess there was something wrong because we have a mask that we wear. We don't want to bring attention to ourselves, we don't want to be cross-examined and we want minimum stress and aggro. You may be in a meeting when you sense an attack coming on, and the more you try to restrain it the more powerful the feelings become, until feeling like you're about to burst you politely excuse yourself before charging out of the door blurrily seeking a comfort zone. So scared and yet so very, very brave.

I became a stranger to myself; someone had moved into my body and was sitting up in the attic of my mind in a rocking chair creaking back and forth. I was not Rachael. I was something else. No energy, no desires, no feelings, no hopes, no life force. Each day after my children had left for school I would sit with my arms draped over the balcony and literally stare into space. I lost all track of time and place and anything, I was barely existing. The balcony was a 'safe zone'. As I mentioned earlier, I had my safe places, safe body positions and comfort zones. By draping my upper body over the balcony I was supported and my muscles did not spasm so much. Plus I could gaze into the gray oblivion and nobody would disturb me.

Anyway, the neighbor would drive to work and then come back for lunch and then go back to work and be back in the evening and I would still be there. Draped. I was turning into the neighborhood watchwoman. Just there, occasionally shuffling to the loo or to pace, or changing position. But the balcony was a safe zone and it was quiet. From where I sat in the distance I could vaguely see some gray trees, gray sky and gray houses. Mum would come by and talk about work, but I had no interest in listening to anything that included mixing with people or going out. It scared me.

My bed was also a safe zone – it had my pillow and my teddy bear (for decoration only, of course) and I could hunch up on it. There was also a chair in the living room which I could drape on . . . God! What was I? a curtain? Pull yourself together and all that.

To me every morning was the start of another shit day. A day that made me tremble with fear, a day where my thoughts would pick at my mind, scratching it and bruising it. I hated my thoughts. They were always awake before me. They quite obviously didn't believe in having a lie-in.

As soon as I opened my eyes I would be 'scanning' for any weird sensations. Physically getting out of bed, my safe place with blankets and my books all around me, was intimidating. I would snatch my clothes out of the wardrobe and then scuttle off to the bathroom to shower quickly and get dressed. Clothes were the same every day, a baggy t-shirt and black tracksuit bottoms. I never bothered to look in the mirror. Would you want to look in the mirror and see a frumpy miserable cow?

Depression is spoken about as if it's a very secret thing. If depression could be seen it would resemble a long, polished hallway that leads to nowhere. It would be cold and smell musty. I have met people over the past few years who are dealing with a nervous illness and they all have a very tense air about them. It's a terrible struggle – no, a battle – to hold on to your emotions as they thud about inside you.

Depression is not a quiet illness. It's very, very loud. It is powerful and unforgiving and it deafens you. It is also a liar and you, in your weakened state of mind, believe what it is saying. It stirs negative emotions inside you and draws you into its world of nightmares and hopelessness. It takes you to a place and binds you into submission. It's a constant presence that causes you to feel only despair and fear. At other times it causes you to feel absolutely nothing, it steals away all your good thoughts, all your hopeful thoughts – anything that will make you contented and peaceful – and it leaves you in a vacant sad place with such little resilience or resistance that sometimes you wonder if you are really here: and then there are the days when you wonder why you are here. What the fuck is it all about?

People trying to cope with depression constantly feel that they are a nuisance and that they are stupid and selfish. In fact they believe anything negative, and because they are so tuned in to this repetition of nasty thoughts and awful feelings they find it very difficult to listen to what the outside world is trying to tell them. As far as they are concerned, there is no way out and they deserve it. I felt I deserved 'it'.

Journal entry: Am goin' to have shower hope I come back.
I have no sense of reason when this madness comes,
Everything is one dark road full of mathematical sums
I try to find a logic,
A reasonable way out,
But all my calculations
Are wrong and make me shout
I add another problem
Subtract a piece of mind
Divide it all together
And hell is what I find.

After waking up, the 'balcony sittings' would start, all day, every day, and if the monster came along I would battle with it and pace around the house in blind agitation. I never answered the phone, which would mean talking. I could not handle talking. The monster always came, of course: it never ever missed a day. You would have thought it could have given me a day off, surely? Weekends or something?

I was lucky that I had a home help, a scrawny little Indonesian lady called Bibit. A devout Muslim who liked nothing better than talking about the time she had won a religious poetry competition in Indonesia and would then duly recite the winning piece to me, hand gestures and all.

Had it not been for Bibit I am pretty sure that my husband and children would have been living in a pigsty, for I had neither the urge nor the inclination to do anything that resembled housework. This from a woman who hated dust and would at one time spend hours cleaning the bathrooms until they shone and sparkled. My mother-in-law once said 'you could sleep on Rachael's bathroom floors'. I was lucky, I appreciate that now. Living in the Far East it is common to have home helps, or amahs as they are called, but for the majority of housewives who go to work and look after their family, trying to cope with anxiety or depression is a bloody nightmare. So much is expected of them and they valiantly struggle on. I don't know how they do it.

Mums who are struggling with a nervous illness seem to have an inbuilt sense of loyalty and dedication. They simply feel that if they don't do it, nobody else is capable, and they look upon motherhood and being married as a duty they must fulfill. We mothers have 'a way' of roasting chicken, 'a way' of making the beds, 'a way' of arranging the cupboards and the fridge . . . at least I did. And it came to the point when I let it all go, I just had to. It wasn't that bad. Life went on. The chicken was not as good as mine but at least edible and the beds looked very abstract with a Spiderman bed sheet and tulip motif design pillowcases but the world didn't stop. We all coped.

So, any Mums out there, let go for a while. The chicken will be fine and sod the bathrooms for today. There has to be a point when you must say 'I need to go a little easier on myself here, I am not a saint and I am not happy.'

Whatever little, tiny solutions help you, go for them. No matter how silly they may seem, how irrational, pathetic or whatever else they seem. You must be true to yourself. It's not easy though, confronting those hidden truths that sway around inside you all day, the ones that make your tummy feel nervous and that make you sit and stare into space juggling them around in your head without finding any answers. Worrying about things you are *convinced* are going to happen and picturing all the negative outcomes which usually involve you being convicted as the worst person on earth.

I was good at that. Straining to be perfect and in control and yet falling apart behind closed doors and crying into my pillow until my face became blotchy and red and there were no more tears left inside me. Ache after ache I would store away and lock them up . . . pain after pain, fear after fear . . . all stuffed inside me bursting at the seams and pushing to get out.

There was an 'outside' and an 'inside' Rachael, and the inside one had a lot to deal with. She was whining and moaning in pain and I ignored her totally. I didn't want anyone to see me break. It was my personal war. I left her alone regardless of what she was trying to tell me. I wasn't listening. She was too awful to listen to.

Journal entry: Anxiety starts off as a possibility in the depths of our brain. Then it nudges our body into action . . . 'Run! Run! Run! Quick!' It shrieks. But where do you run to? It then becomes a physical pain, breathlessness, dizziness, pounding chest, fear all around and nothing to point a finger at.

Chapter Six

'How are you doing?'

Journal entry: If it happens in a public place I have a dreadful urge to run away, or hide. I start to tremble, I need to run, the pain throbs on and I don't know what to do . . . I just keep a 'normal' look on my face but inside I am a wreck. It's like every sinew of muscle in my body has been tugged back into a tense tightness and to relax causes the muscles to be released into spasms of pain.

Mr. Jadish looked expectant, almost as if he was hoping I would say 'Fabulous! Let's do lunch.' I just mumbled 'OK-ish.'

'OK, well, by now you should be noticing a difference,' he said, still staring at me. 'It's been over a fortnight, so . . . anything?' He gave another expectant little smile, the kind a children's television programme presenter uses.

You know when you lie and your eyes kind of flicker and your face kind of feels embarrassed and thick? Well, I reckoned that he *knew*. He *knew* I was not taking the medication and he *knew* I had been lying. Didn't he? I was in a fix. I mumbled and fumbled around a bit, looked at the wall, at the chair, at my shoes, at his shoes . . . not the hush puppies today, I observed. 'Oh what the fuck,' I thought. 'He thinks I'm mental anyway, what have I got to lose? Well, actually I read in this book I have at home that those tablets kind of make you feel bad so I stopped taking them.'

There was a silence, a very heavy silence. Mr. Jadish sort of frowned and did a little sigh, but to give him credit, he soon pulled himself together even though he probably wanted to wallop me. 'You see Rachael' – he took a deep breath, pulled himself up in his chair, lips pursed.

'Oh-oh,' I thought to myself, 'serious talk coming up.'

'Every medication has *possible* side-effects . . . I say possible because not everyone will experience them, there may not be any, but the manufacturers have an obligation to inform the public, plus, the benefits far more exceed the possible side-effects. If, of course there were any.'

He paused, a dramatic pause. I know that because I did A level theatre studies and there are different kinds of pauses. His was *definitely* dramatic.

'Plus,' he continued, 'they are usually very minor. It's rather like having a jab, you know, you get slight symptoms of flu or aches but they come and go very rapidly.'

'Oh puleeeez,' I thought to myself. I *knew* that pills prescription book was not lying! I read it every day: it was sacred and true. This of course was a trick to get me drugged up and manageable. He was a good salesman, but I wasn't buying.

I knew I was coming across as a wuss, a wet blanket, pathos on legs, but . . . I felt fragile, breakable and the anxiety was always humming under my skin and making my muscles vibrate and twinge. I knew he was displeased and rather disappointed because he had believed me, I knew! I knew! Still, he didn't give up on me. Instead he suggested another medication, similar but different. Go figure. It was getting good reviews and he strongly recommended that I did *not* get my little book out but just take a leap into the unknown and go for it. Of course, the monster logic told me that I was already in the unknown – hell, I was living in it.

Pills duly dispensed in little white bags and another appointment made, I went back and immediately got my pill book out. I had to hand it to him, it was difficult to find because it had various brand names, but I found it. Pretty much the same side-effects but sounded OK-ish, or was it? It was also an antidepressant and I know those things can work against you. Like my little pink Xanax®, I took a nibble off the end of one and scrunched it into my drawer. I had quite a selection by now.

Sitting on my bed, I wondered if I was the only person in the world going through this and what I had done that was so bad to be punished by God? I was still trying to remember if there were any particularly supersize sins I had committed. And in God's books what qualified as big? Would it get worse? Was it a long-term thing? Was there anything that was going to make me feel better ever again?

Journal entry: I am intelligent enough to realize that I am highly strung and that my nerves have become over-sensitized.

I'd like to go away
But I doubt that I would find
Any peace at all because
I'd have to take my mind.
My mind is very cruel,
It always brings me down
It hates to see me happy

And is causing me to drown.
My mind is pure hell,
It makes me cower ... Meek
I have already lost it once
Yet without it I grew weak ...
My mind is temperamental
It's never in one mode,
It gives me much to carry,
An overburdened load ...
I hate you mind, I hate you!
Just see what I've become,
A Coward of society,
No use to anyone.
I hear you mind ... Your laughter ...
You're sneering, how you snide ...
Your ever-present torture of my soul,
Where you forcefully reside.
(Happy poem of November 2001)

My pulse is 80 and I am just on edge now, waiting. I am
scared and nervous. Some mornings I'll wake up around 4 or
5. Tense and in pain. Then I'll feel unsettled and too
scared to relax. Each pain sends me into panic. Then I
tense up and wait. Imagining the worst. Fearing the consequences. The pains range from bosom pains, chest tight,
midriff pulls, sore, burning ... at lunchtime had pains in
my throat. Lay feeling my pulse. Lots of fear. Got taken to
the ER for an ECG. Staff all know me now.

Am not sleeping well. Fidgety sleep. Wide awake at 3 ish,
can't sleep with light off. Every day has a pattern. The
same one. Perhaps, no, definitely there is a reason, if only
a small reason ... but maybe it will make a big difference

I don't know why, but one day I decided to start taking the new pills. I was getting to the point where I had nothing to lose. I was a shaking, breathless cow with a problem and I was rapidly spiraling into Neverland. It was an effort to put that little orange tablet in my mouth, one little orange tablet. But I did. Three times daily, I swallowed the pills and ten times daily I had monster attacks.

Nothing was working. I persevered, however, sticking them into my mouth every day, but after ten days I gave up. I was feeling sick, dizzy and scared. I blamed the pills. It might not even have been the pills, but I had to blame something, so I stopped. There was no rationalizing with me at this point. I had no guidelines and my psychiatrist had no idea what I was going through. Nobody did. On this whole planet I was the only woman going through this and I hated it.

Journal entry: Mum took me to see a yoga teacher who specializes in holistic medicine. I was given a 'remedy' to try and my pulse was taken. Everybody was very nice and looked healthy.

At the yoga center I had to lie down on a bed while various 'pressure points' were pressured – arms pulled up, legs massaged, it was very much a 'heads, shoulders, knees and toes' examination. I explained how I had been feeling and also how I was concerned that I had some physical illness as I was experiencing breathlessness, dizziness, palpitations and pains in my chest, legs, stomach, neck, spine and head. There had to be something there that he could cure.

At this point it turned rather weird. After I had finished rattling off my various symptoms the yoga man, who I must say was an exceedingly sympathetic listener, proceeded to turn his attention to my big toe. That's right. My big toe. He squeezed it and pinched it, poked it and rubbed it, his face about half an inch away wrapped in total concentration on this one toe. I have to say I did feel rather uncomfortable. I mean, it's hardly what one expects really is it? To have your big toe be the center of attention when you've come in complaining of breathlessness? Was I missing something here? He wasn't some foot fetish person was he? Perhaps there was some secret chakra point I had overlooked? Perhaps the answers to my ailments lay in my big toe? Gosh, I hoped my feet didn't smell.

Inspection over, the Yogi Bear man smiled and informed me that my 'blood pressure and circulation' was fine. Right. Now, had my big toe told him all this? I made a mental note: 'Make more time to chat with big toe on a daily basis.' 'Your big toe is hairy,' he announced for the whole room to hear, 'hairy toes are a good sign of blood circulation, so no problem there.'

There we are then. They say you learn something new every day, and apart from being painfully aware that the whole room and half the building knew I had a fat hairy big toe, it was apparently a good thing. Wear your hairy toes with pride. Flaunt them for the world to see. Who needs doctors when your big hairy toe can tell you all you need to know about your blood pressure? Just for the record, my big toe is not exactly carpet pile central. It's just a normal, fuzzy cute little big toe. I mean, I don't have to shave it or anything.

Next on the agenda was a massage. The yoga man's daughter poured out some essential oils, and rubbed them into my temples. I do like head massages and attempted to relax: however, I did find myself occasionally opening my eyes to check if her Dad was lurking anywhere around my feet. She was telling me all about the different essential oils – ylang ylang, citronella, lavender, rose and their different properties. Mum looked on expectantly, like a miracle was about to take place and I would 'arise' from the bed declaring I was 'healed, had seen the light and get me a mat and glass of lentil juice'.

I was also shown how to do a yoga position which involved sitting on the floor with one finger on the side of my nose pressing gently on my nostril while taking deep breaths. The yoga teacher showed me what to do and then suggested that I go and sit in the main hall and 'practice' for ten minutes. My sisters do yoga but I have never really 'got it'. (Back in the eighties I remember my Dad would stand on the balcony in his underwear 'saluting the sun', which must have been an interesting experience for any house guests that happened to be staying.) Sitting on the floor at the yoga center with my finger pressing my nostril and with people walking around didn't really help me. I just remember feeling an idiot and I was also concerned that from a distance it might look like I was sitting there casually picking my nose.

I was also told to fast and to make a concoction of beetroot, carrot and apple juice – I think there might have been a potato in there as well so I could possibly have churned up a good old Irish stew. Then there was valerian root, which when I got home I immediately looked up in my herbal remedies book and found to be a distant relation of deadly nightshade. That shook me a little bit. The scariest thing of all, though, was that I had to 'shop' for the items. There was only one nearby supermarket and parking there was awful, so my husband had to wait in the car. He gave me an encouraging smile and said 'Just try.'

I wanted to be brave. I needed to show him that I was OK, and I desperately didn't want confrontation and to appear silly – but this was something I did not want to do. All I had to do was go into a supermarket and get some bloody beetroots, but to me it signified danger. It meant going into a public place where there would be people and I might meet someone I knew and have to talk and what if an attack came on?

All these points had to be taken into consideration. Like a well-planned military operation, you cannot overlook the smallest detail or you will be ambushed and taken prisoner. I scurried in like a lost rabbit, hands shaking, teeth chattering, breathing rapid gulps of air and I felt so fuzzy that I could barely read the shopping list.

'Hello Rachael, shopping?' came a cheerful voice out of the fog.

'Oh fuck.'

It's always the way, just when you do not want to make small talk, someone is there making bloody small talk. Monster just laughs and speeds up the jitter machine. I made a strained effort 'focus on your words, sound intelligent, don't rush, don't fidget,' says one voice, but the other is stronger. 'You are falling apart! Something is coming for you! You are trapped now . . . the pains are getting worse. You are suffocating Rachael! Suffocating!' My chest was twanging, my breathing was thin and I needed oxygen. I was agitated and just wanted to chuck the shopping basket down and flee. In a situation like this I was helpless and my legs felt like they were going to give way any second, but I was under pressure to talk back and to look normal. 'Run, run, and run!' You hear yourself screaming . . . 'You cannot handle this!! Get out! Escape!'

Inwardly I was psyching myself up for war. A very big war. Where was it? Where should I run to? 'The enemy is around but you can't see it. Be on guard Rachael, be on guard!' Somehow, I managed to get through the little suffocating chat, grab the vegetables and charge out of the supermarket practically stumbling to where the car was parked. Sweat was pouring down my face and my breathing was erratic and uncomfortable, my husband knew by now that asking me if I was OK was not a good idea but still . . .

'OK? Mmm? OK?' He rubbed my shoulder.

'Umph' was the only reply I could manage at that point.

As far as I was concerned I had just escaped from enemy territory and was lucky to be alive. I clutched my bag of beets and potatoes, they were fine. 'The eagle has landed.' It eventually peaked, of course, breathing was easier and the humming nerves quietened down. They never completely quieten down though, do they? There is always an incessant buzz reminding you of their presence. It was only temporary relief. I knew that. By the way, the only enlightenment I got from fasting and drinking pureed vegetables was that beetroot juice tastes like liquid sandal.

Journal entry: Earlier on I had that awful pain in my back again. Looked up Gall bladder, peptic ulcer ... pancreatitis ... I'm like a tightly wound spring. I have had a particularly bad day today, I feel like two metal hands are gripping my shoulders. My body, especially my shoulders feel very sore and tense, am getting the pickled-onion claw twinge in my gullet plus breast pain twinges. Am on constant alert for the pains which inevitably come. My brain feels, or rather I feel like my brain is in a barbed wire cage. Mottled and braced. Grey park at the end of a cul-de-sac dead-end road. Had a scary hour today; a wallop of a 'stone, pickled-onion holder' like pain erupted in my middle and is currently throbbing in my stomach ... Today I had a spasm in my throat, I felt unnerved by this but managed to convince myself it was throat muscle tension ... self talk is good ... but that small twang really upset me. Woke up with a jolt. Tense and uncomfortable. Chest feels tight and anticipating something awful happening.
Am about to die ... trouble breathing, feel smothered, feel suffocated, very scared ... like the breath is being squeezed out of me. May have a popped lung. My body is cold and my chest feels tight. May be staring death in the face.

Around this time we moved house. It's said that moving house can be a traumatic experience and indeed the whole idea of packing up and cleaning and driving back and forth with furniture and boxes seemed a mammoth task and I wanted nothing to do with it.

'Where to put the table Ma'am?' the movers asked as I stared at them in a glassy haze. 'The computer? The cups? What about the laundry basket?' I just stood there. The move went on around me. *So much* was expected of me. Who gives a toss where the settee goes? Sod off! Leave me alone. I need peace. It was too much. I was on tenterhooks, I was in constant panic mode and it was clawing at my nerves and manifesting as anger. Why on earth was I being asked to tell them where to put everything? Could they not see?

Bad huh? I sound awful, I was awful, I didn't want to be. I was just zonked and functioning in a place where enemies were lurking, therefore I was aggressive and short-tempered. They were nice men, everyone was nice. And no, it wasn't their fault at all. But I bet they wondered who the hell that strange woman was, who preferred to sit hunched up, arms draped over the back of an armchair with a tense, tight look on her face, and why she hardly spoke but just growled occasionally.

By this time even driving was difficult for me as I was scared to be out on my own. This was a minor form of agoraphobia. According to my *Pears Medical Encyclopedia* I had developed a 'fear of public places'. In actual fact I believe that the fear was not so much about being out in public but of having a panic attack in public. I was scared to go into a shop in case I had an attack or worse, had an attack while talking to somebody.

See, we become very adept at hiding the monster. We are able to appear to be functioning normally while inside we are hanging on with bloodied fingers to a sharp cliff. Speaking to people agitated me, their voices annoyed me. Attempting to have a conversation would bring on all kinds of unhappy sensations. I would be focusing so much on my thoughts and body that I could barely understand what the other person was saying. I would stand there, trying to keep my balance while secretly shaking and in panic mode with a mask-like expression on my face.

The shopping that I did do was done in a rush; I would drag the children around and zoom out of there as fast as possible. Daily life was starting to become hell. My family life was beginning to suffer. My children agitated me and I felt guilty but helpless. My husband did not seem to have a clue what to do. I had become a strange person to him. From a loud, energetic woman I had turned into a shuffling, hunched-up monkey person who lived in a world of her own. I would be doing something and a weird feeling would start to come on, heralding monster's arrival, then I would feel anxious and agitated and if there was a muscle spasm in my chest I would be paralyzed with fear.

I tried to read books about positive thinking, natural remedies, yoga etc., and many a fear-stricken night was spent concentrating on my solar plexus – wherever the hell it was. It felt like my brain was too ill to digest or even attempt anything, it was going too fast and I could not retain information. Then the books started to annoy me. They were too airy-fairy. All these 'expert' opinions written by people who had probably never even experienced anxiety. If they had then they surely would have known that even turning a page took effort, let alone deciphering the words 'serotonin reuptake inhibitors'. They were not understanding and too impersonal.

How could I sit and meditate when I was too jittery to even function? Besides, by then I had diagnosed myself with a blood sugar disorder and was religiously taking notes. I was a maniac with a mission, convinced I could find the magic pill. I knew I had gone too far when one day, having come across some symptoms which I could identify with I diagnosed myself with a prostate disorder. Possible, I thought.

I started to feel that this was an unsolvable problem. People have problems, sure they do – no money, no job, bad love affairs and sad feelings – but they're able to dig deep down into their souls and get a bit of hope or make some sense out of their problems. In my case I felt that I had killed all sense and hope and besides, I had very little hope to begin with.

Writing this, I look and sound so selfish, I know, it's awful. You know how when you panic you become scared, agitated and snappy? If you lose your wallet or you're running late and stuck in a long traffic jam? Imagine you are in a really stressful situation and then imagine feeling like that almost all day long. That stressful agitation and fear simultaneously gnawing at you. That's it. Exhausting.

My husband and I were now sleeping in separate rooms. It was partly my fault and, dare I say this, partly his. My fault because I was virtually non-communicative and morose. The bed was after all a safety zone for me and his presence was like an invasion. I needed to be angled in a particular fashion on the bed, with my books and teddy bear. His being there did not fit in and, as for being intimate and cuddling up, I was concerned I would have a panic attack or a spasm, and was not in a state of mind to be doing a 'Do you think I'm sexy?' routine. Intercourse – whether social or sexual – was not on my agenda. I was no longer a woman. I was a sack of nerves.

And how was it his fault? Because I felt that he was undermining my suffering and that he was not taking it seriously or listening. I tried to explain my feelings and sensations but he still simply didn't get it. He was in denial. He had lost me and did not know where to start looking. Perhaps he thought that by being dismissive and not allowing me to wallow, he was helping. He wasn't, though. I needed to wallow like a hippo in mud. I needed to talk about my pains and thoughts. I needed him and he was not there. As for my children, well, they were all very little. Azim was eight, Dani was seven, Qawi was four and Bazil almost one, noisy naughty little men who needed their Mummy and yet were noticing that Mummy was not 'very well'. I did my best though. I would give them baths and make play-dough for them, but on bad days I would ask Mum to have them for a while. It was the agitation that got to me the most. I would be ready to snap at anything.

Journal entry: Yesterday was awful. broke down in tears at the ER. I felt scared and helpless and alone . . . what carried me through? Resignation. I think God hates me a lot.

Chapter Seven

Angels in strange places

⭐ ⭐ ⭐

Journal entry:
If I had a prayer
I'd pray for inner strength,
I'd pray for knowledge,
I'd pray for you
I'd pray for me
I'd pray . . .
If I had a prayer.

I think everyone has a bit of obsessive–compulsive disorder in them. You have a desire, an urgency to check you have locked the door, you know you have but your mind tells you to check it again (and again), or you cannot relax until you have straightened the curtain or a picture on the wall – it has to be just so. I remember when I was at school in England and was walking back to my house at boarding school. It was snowing and a freezing day as I trundled up-hill laden with bags and books. It would take about ten minutes to walk from class to my house and I couldn't wait to get back and thaw out my semi-frozen toes. I was almost there when I suddenly had a strong feeling that I had to walk back and touch the lamppost not far from class. It was miles away, but the feeling persisted: it was forcing me to go back and if I did not touch the lamppost at least eight times then something 'bad' would happen to my family. I did it. I had to. I was 'obsessively compulsed' to do it and there ain't no reasoning or rationalizing in that. I was trying to control my world through fol-lowing certain patterns of behavior. If I could not don a cape and wear my underwear inside out then I would have to save the world by being a victim of OCD. So you can imagine how bloody thrilled I was when I became all OCDish again during my anxiety attacks. Yup, I became obsessed about controlling my life and its surround-ings. I was paranoid that bad things would happen and therefore I would be forced to ensure that everything around me was in order.

Good old obsessive–compulsive disorder. I was forced to count the number of times I turned off the bathroom light, I had to turn over in bed at least twenty times, I had to touch the corner of the drawer . . . and to my tired and stressed-out mind these imaginary orders were real. They had to be followed – if I did not carry out these instructions something bad would happen. I was responsible. It's a bit like not stepping on the cracks on the pavement. My mind was so vulnerable it believed anything. It accepted anything which it thought to be true.

Well, let me tell you, switching a lamp off and on twenty times ain't gonna save the world, it only wastes electricity and no matter how much your brain niggles at you to listen, don't! We're at the mercy of our thoughts and as far as we're concerned there is no other way to be – but there is. I never realized this at the time. I was compelled to keep an orderly structure: I felt more in control that way. So there it was, another package of delights unraveling in my head. Glory be. I'm turning into a lunatic.

One morning I woke up and shuffled into the kitchen where my home help Bibit had to hold my shaking hand as I attempted to drink a glass of water. It had been a bad night with spasms and sweats and nightmares. I felt like shit in a blender. In my diary I had scrawled 'am in hell'. There was a tight iron band around my body and I was shaking. Everything was surreal and far away, I was drowning in space and struggling to breathe. I crawled to the phone and dialed my husband's office, whispering for him to take me to the doctor's. Then I sat and went through the motions of the monster attack, but this one was bad. It was overtaking me. What should I do? I paced, oxygen was not there, I opened the door and huddled over the balcony, not working. I was getting scared and whimpering.

Bibit brought in a cup of tea and stood by helplessly. She was tearful and told me to calm down, sshhh, ssshh . . . She stroked my hair and patted my shoulder whispering '*sabar Bu*' ('patience Ma'am', in Malay). I felt bad for her. She didn't know what was happening to me. Unfortunately, that made two of us.

I was about to die. I felt it. This was the real thing. I was dying a slow death and God was not around. I wanted my Mum, I wanted to be safe, I wanted my boys, I wanted to be little and playing outside on the swing. I wanted safe. Where was safe? How could I find it? How could I hide from the monster of death? By the time my husband arrived I was a muddle of nerves, hardly recognizable and I told him that my stomach hurt. I was still trying to pretend. I had to say something that made sense to the outside world and to say the monster was attacking me and trying to take my life was not logical. What 'monster'? Hello?

This time I went to another family doctor – a very nice man who took one look at me and said 'Oh dear.' Without being asked I immediately clambered onto the gurney in his office, hunched up on all fours commanded him to call an ambulance. 'I need to be admitted,' I sobbed. What happened next was a vague flurry of telephone calls to a private medical center followed by having to listen to my husband lecture me in the car. 'You are all right, why are you doing this? You are being stupid! You are OK, sit up! Why are you sitting hunched up?' I know he was worried and concerned and felt totally helpless but so did I, and all the shouting in the world would not, could not alter my state of quivering brain. I had no thoughts, just fear. No rationalizing please, I am a goner. Thus, with my head almost submerged in the dashboard and my hands clutching the seat I was taken with great speed to see another set of doctors, nurses and specialists.

All I knew at that time was that I could not breathe. I was screaming with fear, it was tearing around inside me, pounding and clawing and scratching. I felt like physically digging my brain out and throwing it on the motorway. That's how bad it was.

At the medical center I was put in a wheelchair and left alone while the nurses filled in my details. Sitting in the wheelchair I had a huge attack. The air was getting thinner and I felt dizzy. I called to a nurse and grabbing her hand I told her to stay with me because I couldn't breathe. She looked puzzled but duly walked me up and down the reception area. She was not a great help; I remember thinking that, in fact I could have got more comfort from talking to the wheelchair.

Eventually it peaked. To those of you who know the peaked feeling, isn't it liberating? You have been set free again and for a brief second, minute, hour or even a whole day, you feel OK. It's like a gush of clear water in your mind. It sparkles and soothes but is soon gone.

After the peak I felt able to go and get myself a hot drink from the vending machine down the hall. It was not far away and I felt I could manage it, but as soon as I got there another attack came on and I had to hunch over. I looked like I was trying to stand on my head. I was wearing really ugly slippers and my hair was greasy. I looked like 'er indoors, about to scrub the front step. Plus I have an ample bottom. It's hereditary and kind of the main part of my anatomy. Anyway, I was screwed. Upside down in bad slippers having a monster moment. Shit, so the experts say, happens, and it was happening now.

From a distance I heard someone approaching, someone in clicking heels and a nice perfume, who had stopped and someone who was now standing right there next to me.

'Hello,' said a voice, 'are you all right?'

Oh no! Not a question! (Clearly the fact I was standing upside down in a compromising position wasn't giving any clues here.) Nor could I say that I was the vending machine repairwoman. I was blurry and struggling, the floor seemed very far away and I had a question to answer. I managed to bring my head up high enough to see a very tall, attractive lady with blonde hair standing there. Very arty, early fifties with a colourful scarf draped around her shoulders.

'Sorry, I can't stand up,' I mumbled, 'having bad attack of breathlessness and I feel panicky.' There was a silence as she was obviously trying to work out what I had just said. 'She thinks I'm a weirdo,' I remember thinking.

'Oh dear.' She sounded sympathetic. 'You poor thing. I know all about those kinds of feelings . . . I used to get them when I was younger, awful things, dreadful, but you will be all right.'

Will be all right? The sheer presumptuousness of this casual statement! Idiot! Didn't she get it? How could I be all right? I was suffering! I had been personally picked out by God to suffer! I was the original sinner and had been found, tried and sentenced to a life of unlife. She probably thought I was a drug addict suffering from withdrawal symptoms. The 1970s was, after all, her era – the time of liberation and magic mushrooms, when women burnt their bras and looked at their vaginas and had monologues with them. Gosh, I hope she didn't think that's what I was doing, bent over and such.

Look lady, if you're going to assume I'll be all right kindly keep it to yourself because all right is not on the agenda here. I didn't say this – of course I didn't say it – but my agitated self was surfacing and I knew she was only trying to be helpful plus I *was* blocking her from getting a cup of coffee. So I stayed hunched up with a pathetic attempt at an amicable smile on my face wondering if I should run off down the hall shouting 'the bells . . . the bells!' to prove I was a lost cause.

'Yes,' she was saying while trying to reach over me to press the chococappucino button. 'I will *never* forget my first panic attack . . . I was at the hairdressers and . . .' Whoa there! Panic attack? She knew about panic attacks? That's what they were called?

'Bloody awful,' she was saying 'and at that time not much was known about them. Horrendous . . . made you feel like you were suf-focating, always scared and agitated.' But there was nothing to be scared of, she assured me. 'You see it's just in your mind, and that's what you have to repeat to yourself, you scare them off instead.'

By now I was standing up kind of straight and grabbing this opportunity she zapped the button and got her coffee, obviously mindful that I might decide to hunch up again or hunch up and block her access to the machine. We're so unpredictable.

'But it's like I am about to die,' I whispered.

'Well you won't, it's just a feeling, don't fight it, and besides, you can't be afraid of dying, it's just another beautiful journey to look forward to one day. I promise you, you are going to be fine.' I wasn't so sure about the dying being a beautiful journey part, but here was something to think about . . .

She looked so convincing and was so nice. Her name was Eleanor and she was in Brunei for a brief visit. We exchanged addresses and then she said goodbye and breezed off down the hall, leaving a lovely scent of flowery blossomy perfume in the air and a little bit of hope behind her. Hope.

On that day, at that moment, Eleanor was my angel. It sounds corny I know, but she was. She had turned up when I was swimming in cement, she had helped me in a time of morbid fear and I am eternally grateful to her. She gave a name to the monster – panic attack. That's what it was called! It didn't seem a fierce enough name somehow. 'Rabid, brain-destroying, soul-sucking demon' – or panic attack.

The sheer relief and comfort I experienced when she told me that she too had experienced them was beyond description. Who would have imagined that there, at a vending machine, in this beautiful medical center situated on the island of Borneo I would have met someone who *knew*? Magic words! I was not the only one! I was not the only one who had met the monster. It obviously had a network out there, all ready to move in on unsuspecting victims and slowly destroy them. How was I going to stop them? (Where *is* Flash Gordon when you need him?)

Journal entry: I am so overwrought with fear and panic that I don't focus and become highly agitated and snappy. Is my heart diseased or ill at ease? It could strike at any moment . . . so much to handle.
Oh cruel abandonment of faculties,
Yet again you have taken flight,
Subjecting me to misery, to fearfulness and fright . . .
Oh cruel, cruelest predicament
So much for one to bear
Afraid of day, afraid of night,

Does anybody care?
Neglected by my sanity,
Rejected by my mind,
The smallest piece of peace I had
I can no longer find.
I'm reaching out to nothing
A prayer or a wing,
I crawl along this graveled path,
What will tomorrow bring?

My room at the medical center was beautiful: had I been in a clearer state of mind I would have appreciated the ocean view through the bay windows. Palm trees swaying in the breeze and a clear sunlit sky . . . a canopy of different blues. There was a TV with access to dozens of channels, a lovely fruit display of huge plump orange mangoes, strawberries and grapes. Who cared? Nothing else was OK.

The bathroom was magnificent too – gleaming marble tiles, a walk-in shower behind clouded glass doors, gold faucets, fluffy white towels and bathrobe with slippers . . . all very *The Bold and the Beautiful*. Lovely, but they could have stuck me in a broom cupboard and I wouldn't have noticed.

Picture the scene . . . me in an elegant white bathrobe, delicately caressing a flute of Dom Perignon while gazing out at the ocean and suddenly 'he' would enter . . . Dr. Kildaire. 'Hello Rachael,' he would whisper almost inaudibly, overcome by the sight of my curvaceous silhouette subtly outlined in the orange glow of the setting sun. I would not turn round but merely murmur 'So, you came.' That's how glamorous that place was – very Hollywood. Actually, on second thoughts maybe Keanu Reeves would enter. . . . No, Colin. Colin Firth. (I love Colin Firth.)

Life is so unfair – all this luxury and no mind to appreciate it. In fact the best thing about the whole idyllic scenario was there. Outside shimmering in the sun . . . a beautiful and elaborately designed balcony. This meant I could lean and hunch as much as I wanted! I opened the doors and draped myself over it like a wet towel. An intense panic was starting to come over me and I felt oxygenless, for want of a better word. The palms were doing their swaying, the sea was gently sparkling and I was gasping for breath. I tried to distract myself and looked at the sky, the sand, the bits of granite on the floor . . . but I was trying too hard, and the more I tried to distract myself the more intense it became.

'It's just a feeling,' I told myself, 'ignore it.' I remembered Eleanor's words. I was fighting a feeling. My mind was functioning at cross-purposes: it would deal with the stronger feeling first and react to it. I was like a wild jungle animal, flared nostrils, adrenaline pumping, heart beating. Clinging to the balcony at a five-star medical center I hung on for dear life and waited for it to peak.

I wondered what the doctors could do for me at this plush place. It was super efficient and the nurses looked like stewardesses and were all slim and pretty, but they didn't seem to understand. My category of illness didn't fit into the usual appendix, pregnancy, broken leg section – I had a broken brain and a plaster wouldn't fix that. They tested my blood and urine and then I was taken to the gym where a Barbie look-alike tested my lung capacity. This was a process whereby I had to blow into what looked like a giant bellow. Yes, a giant bellow.

They whizzed me around smooth, plant-lined corridors that smelt of disinfectant. I looked awful and felt rather ugly to be in such a good looking place. Even the doctor that attended to me looked like he should be in *The Bold and the Beautiful*: Australian, tall, dark curly hair and green eyes and a smile to have a breakdown for. I felt a little easier at being in the medical center, perhaps because it was a safe zone – oxygen masks all around if I fainted and nurses there at the press of a button who would listen to me chatter nervously on about my pains, fears and the throes of being on planet oxygenlessness. Later that night I had another attack and a very pleasant nurse came to sit with me. She was very nice and I am sure I would have felt better had she not chosen to discuss the recent death of a patient, but God she went on about it. It was like being stuck in a scary movie. I'm suffering from anxiety for God's sake. Tell me something happy!

The night wore on, me lying there on my expensive duckdown pillow quietly hyperventilating with a nurse from the twilight zone.

As you may have guessed, I was prescribed more little tablets, and the good-looking doctor was pleased to inform me that I had an appointment with Mr. Jadish (whom he had contacted) the day after I was discharged. I was also told to take it easy and relax. I wish I'd thought of that.

That afternoon Mum came to pick me up, hoping I am sure that I was a bit better. I clutched the seat, hunched up was driven home.

Journal entry: Am trying St. Johns Wort, garlic and licorice supplements. 'You have nothing to fear but fear itself' (F. D. Roosevelt).
'Fear of Fear = Fear' Rachael Malai Ali.
'I fear this because I deserve it. This is what I deserve because I have nothing left.

In between these bouts came intermissions of brightness and relief. During these times I would cook dinner and play with my children. I smiled as much as I could; I wanted them to know I was still here, that I was doing my best to climb back and reach the place where I could function as Mummy and not as this stranger lady. I loved them so much and in their little world the way I was behaving did not make sense. Mummies are fun and smiley, they smell good and they give hugs, they only shout if we are naughty and they play with us. Why is our mummy different now?

On really good days I would sit downstairs under the house and watch the cats playing. Even when I sat down I would have to stretch my body into a very tense taut position, like a rope that could not fray. If I was too relaxed a twinge might come on and I did not want that. I had to be in a defensive mode, the monster could not catch me off guard. Every sinew of muscle in my body felt like it was tugged back but to relax would have caused them to spasm in pain.

Days passed into nights. Nights for me began at shower time. Just before sunset I would have a quick tense shower, and then put my pajamas on. I felt safe in nightclothes. Nighttime was quieter. It was not harassed and there was not a lot of noise. Nighttime may have brought on monster attacks but it was somehow never quite as bad as daytime.

Journal entry: I don't know, I don't know, I don't know, I don't know.

Chapter Eight

I'm a little teapot

Journal entry: I believe I am not meant to be like this. You know, a lot of people think I'm strong and bossy ... but although I may be bossy ... I am not strong. I am struggling with an anxiety disorder and it scares me ... It hurts a lot ... at the end of the day I'm on my own. I have so much to do. My shoulders are weighed down.

Do you ever get the 'I am the worst person in the world' feeling? I did, and still do sometimes. The worst person in the world is very good at belittling themselves; they are plagued by feelings of guilt and worthlessness and feel themselves to be bad. They brainwash themselves with these negative thoughts on a daily basis until they start to believe it. As I said earlier, I believed myself to be the worst mother in the world – I believed anything negative – and eventually, I guess, my fears and beliefs overtook me.

When a person is in the throes of a nervous breakdown every little task seems gigantic. Being nervously ill means you do not want to be disturbed. By this I mean you become antisocial. It's part of the illness – well, it was a large part of mine – because you are dealing with so many thoughts and emotions and sensations within your body that you crave peace and quiet. You become almost catatonic. I used to sit at the dinner table not wanting to be spoken to, I wanted everything over as soon as possible so I could go to my room and read my books hunched up.

At the other end of the scale I did not want to be burdensome. I knew that I was acting strangely and my children were trying to cope with it as well, but I preferred to be alone with no noise and no expectations. For a mother who adores her children this wasn't easy and I tried very hard to be as normal as I could around them, but it was a struggle and I hated myself. There was nothing to pinpoint, no clue as to where the monster came from, it was just there.

I was not angry with anybody except myself. The snapping and scowling were a cover-up. I hated what was happening, and I could see it, but I couldn't stop it. I know how much my family wanted me to be my old self and I was struggling to do that. I knew people meant well and that I should make a little effort, but at that time 'a little effort' meant waiting for the time when the monster was not around – but the monster was *always* around, it was part of me. In effect, it *was* me – I just hadn't realized it yet.

It grew from my emotional frailty, nurtured by my tension and worries, feeding on my problems and fears. It had been inside me for a long time and was now out of control.

Journal entry: OK. I don't know anymore. I am scared to death ... Hardly slept last night, kept waking up and having pains in my body. Hair drenched with sweat. Felt out of sorts.

Welcome listeners one and all,
Now quickly gather round,
Put your ears close to the wall
Hear my head throb and pound.
Am I insinuating torture of a symbolic kind?
I'd prefer to call it a lapse of reason,
A pause within my mind.
(I got very poetic on some days. Quite lovely really if you
are into morose, depressing verse.)

Due to my highly tense state, my muscles were always rigid, especially in my shoulders and my back. I carried myself like a monkey, with one arm slung over my head. I had my own logic for this. By walking ape style I was less prone to chest spasms. My arm stretched over my head was a comfort zone. If I felt tense or stressed I would need to stretch out my body. I felt better like this and more in control.

Much to my family's dismay, I would walk around like that. As for food? Well, I could hardly taste it. There were days that Bibit had to literally feed me, bits of toast and sips of something. My sister Paula took me and Mum out to lunch one day, a lovely restaurant but I sat there just wanting to go home. The menu was full of words, the other customers agitated me and I felt so bad because I knew that Mum and Paula were doing their best to help. Everything tasted like wet cottonwool. Food was all the same. Life was all the same. Nobody could see the colors of my world because there were none.

I was constantly on alert for pains. I became a 'scanner'. Remember the Daleks? I would be constantly scanning for any unusual body aches or spasms. Some may say, 'So what? We all get aches and pains, what's the big deal?' But to a nervously ill person, even the slightest twinge is the last straw on an already over-burdened camel.

We blow it way out of proportion. There is no limit to our morbid imagination. We are on alert for a serious illness with a mind that is constantly churning out pathetic and depressive moods to a feeble body. For a nervously ill person pain makes them feel more power-less, the mind immediately exaggerates it and once again we are frozen with fear. Every time I tried to fight the feelings I would end up more panicky and scared. I was not succeeding. I tried to ignore them, I tried to be brave, I tried everything but to no avail.

Journal entry: In the state of fear we imagine the worst case scenarios:
Headaches: Brain tumour
Numbness: Stroke
Nausea: Cancer
Chest: Heart
Dizzy: About to die.

There's no gray area – your mind accepts this diagnosis as a fact. Not only are you dealing with bodily pain, but you then have to cope with the reaction to the pain, which is morbid fear, and your body goes through all the motions of fear. You're stuck on a roundabout and there's no getting off!

'Have you been taking your pills?'

These were the words that shook me. I liked Mr. Jadish, he was understanding, he asked the right questions and he listened without judging me. OK, he was a psychiatrist but he was a cool guy. When he asked me about the pills I lied. I said yes I had.

He asked how I was feeling and, remembering the side-effects described in my prescription pill book I duly told him I had felt a bit 'nauseous and shaky'. This seemed to satisfy him, and me, until he then told me he would increase the dosage 'slightly'. Bum. The med-ication needed to be in my system for a month or so until it started to take effect and then I would begin to feel better, he explained. Which meant I was way, way behind schedule.

These pills also ended up in my bedroom drawer, as I had once again convinced myself that I was not going to go through the extreme anxiety of coping with side-effects. It was wrong, but to me it felt safer. Nobody knew I wasn't taking the pills. Nobody. I lied to everyone. I had to. I didn't want to take them. They scared me and I didn't want to go through side-effects. Besides, I would have no way of distinguishing what was a side-effect and what was the monster, and what if side-effects were worse than the monster? These were the happy little thoughts that I had to deal with.

Due to my bad eating habits I began experiencing prickly sensations in my upper stomach. These sensations were of course either my bad heart, my ulcer about to erupt or a giant hernia. According to my medical encyclopedia I definitely had an ulcer. The hot acidic pains would get so bad and penetrate through to my back like a knife. One morning, shaking like a leaf, I managed to drive myself to see a private doctor. Sitting in the waiting room was awful; the receptionist asked me some very difficult questions.

'Hello Rachael. How are you?'

Blank. Was this a trick? I stood there wobbling like a giant raspberry-flavored jelly (raspberry is my favorite flavor).

'Which doctor would you like to see?'

I racked my brain.

'How's work?'

Oh for goodness sake, what was this? An interrogation? I didn't know who I wanted to see; I just wanted to see a doctor! She knew the old Rachael, the one that had been there during all four pregnancies, the one that would pop in for flu meds, the one that smiled and wanted to chat. But I was not her at the moment. Inside I was shaking and having a bad time remaining calm. I needed immediate help. Somehow I answered with the nearest Rachael look I could find, and then I went and sat down on the edge of the chair and stared at the clock, secretly taking my pulse.

Eventually after five whole minutes I was called and shuffled in to a welcoming smile from the family doc. I lost it then. I cried and cried and apologized and outlined all my symptoms. He listened. That was good. No funny expressions, no frowns, no dismissive 'just a bit of stress . . . blah, blah' .

'Well, let's see then,' he said and proceeded to do a thorough check up. 'BP normal, heart, bit fast but fine.' Did he say 'HEART A BIT FAST'?

I looked at him: 'Fast?'

'Yes, but it's fine, you are feeling anxious and it's normal for your heartbeat to increase if you feel a little scared or worried.'

Get my symptoms book out later, I thought.

Journal entry: For the past 24 hours have been in hell . . . I am petrified . . . felt out of control . . . I have an awful feeling . . . I reckon I am being punished . . . think I might have gallstones.

Every waking hour I was totally engrossed with my body and my thoughts were muddled. I wasn't seeing any light at the end of the proverbial tunnel. My world was a very rigid place, dark, hopeless and morbid. I was carrying out instructions; trying not to disturb the monster I would tip-toe around my being in a fidgeted, agitated state of mind. The voice of insanity totally blocked out the voice of reason.

Journal entry: Sometimes IGNORING it can be good . . . accept it as a bodily twinge, a tired muscle . . . a headache . . . whatever. My head feels a bit achey . . . too much thinking I guess.

Chapter Nine

Daycare

Journal entry: This morning woke up in a state of hazy, sleep-induced anxiety . . . had weird pains and then went to the bathroom where I proceeded to throw up all of last night's dinner.

Due to my increasingly worsening state of mind, Mum decided a little vacation would be good. She suggested I go and stay with my sister Paula in Malaysia for a few days. Leaning on the work surface in the kitchen trying to cope with a panic attack I nodded and burst into tears. Arrangements were made, my flight was booked and a ticket bought. There was an evening flight and if I hurried and packed I could get on it.

I remember my husband was sitting in the corner of the sitting room with my little son on his knee as I trundled across to say bye and that I would be back soon. Guilt and worry surged in my stomach and up into my throat as I looked at their faces; I was a bad mother and a sad case wife. I kissed them, clumsy guilty kisses, tears running down my face and all the explanations I wanted them to hear locked inside me, unable to get out.

I was to leave for the airport from Mum's house. Sitting in the kitchen as she bustled around, the reality of what I was about to do hit me. I was going to go to a busy airport, stand in a queue to check in and then board a flight on my own. I have been flying since I was five and from the age of thirteen would travel back and forth from boarding school in England. But this was not the same. The thought of going through the process of checking in at a busy airport and then actually sitting in a plane for two hours in this state of mind? It was too much.

The 'what if's?' surfaced. 'What if I feel breathless? What if I get a pain? What if I get the worst panic attack when I am sitting next to a complete stranger? What if I start to cry? What if I want them to turn the plane back? What if I embarrass myself? What if they yell at me? What if I faint?' There was only one thing to do. Not risk it.

I began to get agitated and anxious; Mum's voice was in the background somewhere. I had to escape from this situation, I felt tense and needed to get to a safer place. Not here though – too many questions to answer and too much hassle. My breathing was becoming shallow and fear was slithering around my bones and sucking the life out of me. I had to think of a way to escape.

Grabbing my Mum's car keys, I mumbled that I needed to go to the grocery shop and get some sanitary towels. 'Won't be long,' I said, ignoring her telling me that the flight left in an hour. I was not interested in that, and I was definitely not going to be on it anyway. Distracted and trembling I drove the car to my other safe place, the hospital. Somehow or other I got there and charged in, nearly collapsing at the reception desk . . . and telling them to get a doctor as I was having 'breathing problems'.

By this time, the nurses recognized me and knew what to do. Gently two nurses ushered me into the doctor's waiting room and told me to sit down while they called the matron. Sitting there as people bustled by with my hands clenched and body huddled up I wondered if the matron would get there on time. I was struggling to breathe and was shaking.

'Hey Rachael.' Matron came in. 'What's wrong? Why are you here, hmm?' Matron Halim is a familiar face at the hospital and I have known him a long time. I broke down into sobs and told him there was something wrong with me, 'it was in my head and it was making me not breathe'.

He looked very concerned and said 'It's not like you, you always look so happy.' Yes, probably the *old me* but not *this me*. I asked him to get me a room to rest and did he have anything to help me sleep? I wanted any kind of peace that was on offer and I wanted it now, packaged, bottled whatever. Now!

A room was arranged and then I had the uncomfortable task of watching him phone my mother. In my state of panic I had not realized that I had been at the hospital for over an hour. Such was the state of my mind, so selfish and yet so hurting, how was I ever, ever going to get rid of it? How was I ever going to make people see that I was not happy like this? I did not mean to hurt anyone. I did not want to feel scared all day.

Journal entry: I see no lesson in this fear. I feel like I am being smothered . . . Like I am about to die. I find fear leads to agitation and anger and subsequently everyone gets angry with me. I feel very scared, like I am choking or drowning, anxiety level is 10 plus, I wonder if anyone else out there is feeling the way I am feeling at this very minute, I wish we could hold hands.
'to be or not to be' (plagiarized)

Sitting on the bed I waited for something to happen. Nurses passed to and fro, the ward smelt funny, the bed was hard and I wanted to go home. I was not making sense. My husband and Mum arrived, looking tired and strained and angry and worried. In that moment I saw the effect I was having on them. How awful is that? To not want to be there and yet to not know where I wanted to be.

I started to cry and said 'Sorry, sorry.' Mum was good but my husband was just lost. A few hours ago he had said goodbye to me and thought I was flying off for a break. Well, I had the break and it wasn't a holiday. I was the break. I was broken. And he was feeling broken too.

In my marriage I had always been the boss. I had always assumed responsibility and done as much as I could to look after everyone. Mum stuff and wife stuff. Shouting at dirty socks on the floor, helping with homework (sometimes) going for drives to beaches and talking about our day over dinner. My children and husband were the focus of my attention and I liked that. Although I had a good career, I was a mum and wife, first and foremost. Old-fashioned? I don't think so. I guess my attempt to be over-effective was part of my downfall though. I tried too hard. I wanted the perfect, no hassle, no rents to pay, no worries life. Just like those glossy families in an American housekeeping magazine. I failed to see that nothing is perfect and that I was not going to solve all the problems that came our way.

Marriage especially is a huge gamble. I was only 24 when I was married; I was desperate to prove how excellent a wife I was, that my husband had made the right decision by marrying me. I wanted to score top points for housewifery and mothering. Not that anyone was keeping score apart from me. Just me. Insecure and naive.

Sometimes we cannot understand how much our loved ones suffer. They want to help us but they don't know where to start. They want us to be normal, to laugh, to make them laugh, to do normal things, they feel just as helpless as we do. I never was aware of how much my family put up with. I have a brilliant family. My amazing boys, Mum, my two wonderful sisters and my grandparents . . . all had to put up with me. Love is powerful.

That day in the hospital was a surrender point. I was now a total wreck. Erratic and inconsistent. It was a deciding factor in the next step. Mr. Jadish, who had been called, decided to put me into the day ward of the psychiatric unit. He wanted me to have time away from home and a routine. That was not a good thing. The day ward? Psychiatric unit? Was I being certified? Visions of straitjackets and padded rooms floated in my head; I had seen enough movies to know that this was not good. Not good. Not good. Oh God! I was going to be in a mental ward! Did they actually have my size in straitjackets?

Mum was not happy with this and, for my husband, it was too much. He hated it. He was angry. He was scared. He was concerned. Imagine your partner, the one you love, the one you married, the one you thought you knew and the one you thought you could always be there for ending up in a psychiatric unit? What was going on? Due to my profound ignorance of psychiatric disorders, I too was horrified – but now I know. And it is because of this experience that I realize that a person with a psychiatric illness, be it a nervous disorder, depression, schizophrenia, anything that the eye cannot see and no plaster can heal . . . a person with this kind of illness is a person who is struggling daily with anguish and confusion. I have nothing but the utmost respect for them.

It was like my first day at school: that was how I would describe entering the ward. I said goodbye to my husband and was led in by a very nice male nurse who asked me to 'sign in please Rachael'. That was good – at least they knew I could write. So here I was again, on the defensive, embarrassed and scared not knowing what kind of people I would meet.

I was taken to the day room where nurses were mingling and talking to patients. The nurses were dressed in normal clothes and were only distinguishable as staff by the name tags they wore. It was a long brightly lit room with a table and comfortable chairs, pictures on the walls and there was a big television set. Boxes of board games and jigsaw puzzles were stacked neatly in a corner and magazines and books were scattered around. It did look normal, in fact, rather like the den at my boarding school. I scanned the room looking for potential Jekyll and Hyde characters. Nope, everyone seemed all right.

In fact nobody paid much attention to me. I was asked to sit down, and 'what would I like to do?' Read a magazine? Draw? OK, now that was weird. Did the guy say 'draw'? The nurse looked at me expectantly, obviously not realizing how profoundly silly that question had seemed. I opted for the magazine – a somewhat outdated *Woman's Own*.

My day had begun on a very strange note and I was trying to find the right song. What was expected of me in this place? How was I going to get well reading a magazine? Were they taking notes? Was I being closely observed? Should I behave normally and what *was* normal? In fact, would they know my normalness from my unnormalness? What if when I was actually normal they thought I wasn't?

Was this a test? I began to feel claustrophobic: the magazine was not helping, I felt homesick and wanted out. The windows were high up and I noticed that one of the seemingly quiet patients had started to march up and down the room with his hands behind his back. He had also assumed a rather dignified pose about him and kept stopping to greet everyone. He was heading towards me. Shit!

I attempted to pretend to read the *Woman's Own* flapjack recipe. Obviously not convincing enough as he was right in front of me, standing there and staring with a smile on his face. Call it instinct but I nodded and said 'hello', there was a pause and then he briefly returned my nod and carried on doing his rounds. Mary, one of the nurses leant over and whispered that 'Mr. Jaya has grandiose delusions, he thinks he is a King and is going around greeting his subjects.'

She sounded so casual, as if she was telling me that she had just put the kettle on. I struggled to interpret this information. I knew I could. Give me a sec. 'Grandiose delusions . . . thinks he is a king . . . greeting his subjects. Right.' The windows seemed higher than ever and the door was far away.

I gave a small smile and realized that I was in a place where different worlds unite, and wondered if I should tell her that I could not breathe and I needed to run away? Silently I sat. Scared and more confused than ever. In the distance Mr. Jaya the King was meeting his loyal subjects. Was he in a happier place than me?

Journal entry: I feel absolutely morbid today. I had a really strange clenching feeling around the top of my left bososm, like a tugging claw. I have spent all day in bed as I am too scared to move about . . . the fear is indescribable. I wasn't even thinking about the pain when it just came, sharp knife-like tugs.

hapter Ten

'All the world's a stage, dude ...'

⭐ ⭐ ⭐

Journal entry: The thing about anxiety and Depression is that your Brain, the one thing you depend on to function NORMALLY, has broken down, it's turned against you, Instead of helping you focus and think in a structured manner, it LIES to you. So, where do you go when your brain malfunctions? It's a cruel trick.

All my emotions were slowly surfacing and creeping over me. I was raw. Nothing was hidden from me, all my fears and worries had overtaken my body and I was fighting for release. Medicine, pills, doctors, did nothing. I was alone in this. Nobody truly, truly understands another person's state of mind really. I found this out the hard way.

Sure people will listen and try to sympathize, but unless they were to climb inside me and take a good look they could not fully know what I was experiencing, that was the torment of it. You get a headache you take a pill, you sprain an ankle you get a massage and a bandage, soon it will heal and you feel better. But this? When for God's sake would it stop? How would it go away when I did not even know where it came from?

How could I tell my dear neighbor that her rattling on and on about her plants and the best way to trim bougainvillea was not what I wanted to listen to when I felt like I was about to die? And how could I make my husband understand that I was not in any way being a wuss and I felt like I was trembling to death? As for going out in public . . .

But can't you all see? I am not a well bunny rabbit. Help me but leave me alone. But come back! But listen! But go away! But I am scared. But . . . That was it. Every day, a constant battle of murky, soul-sucking emotional vacuum cleaners that fed on my blood and self and chewed me up and spat me out, until I was a fragile carcass of pity.

My legs were heavy. I would have to walk though, my teeth would be chattering and I would have to talk, my brain was in fuzz mode and I would have to think, my heart was pounding and thundering and I would have to survive. Mount Everest was nothing compared to this mental mountaineering. The blizzards and snow and icy crevices were all in my little one cell of a mind and I was lost in the storm.

Then there was the awful agitation – my senses hurt from all the 'noise' they were exposed to, like when you eat cold ice cream and you hit a nerve in your tooth. Only this was constant. A painful, exposed nervy feeling that was me. My visits to the day room were monotonously boring. The food was damp and the kitchen smelt of stainless steel and medicine. I drew pictures which I was told were 'very, very good Rachael', I became quite competitive and was very happy when one was pinned on the board. I spoke to the other patients until they were taken away for their dose of happiness, after which they would come back and fall asleep in their chairs and I would be left talking to myself, which I guess was all right given where I was.

I got to know a very nice volunteer called Mr. Sigh who was from Malaysia and seemed to understand what I was going through. Sometimes he would take me for a walk and we would discuss life and religion, both of which were an alien concept to me at that stage. The fact that Mr. Sigh spoke *to* me and not *at* me was what I liked about him. We would chat about everything under the sun from children's welfare to chapatti recipes. Perhaps it was his job, to suss me out – I don't know, but he made me feel comfortable to be me and even if I did have an attack, it was OK. I also learnt how to make chapattis: wholewheat flour and water. Make the dough, flatten with your hand and bake.

Nevertheless, I got on well with Mr. Sigh and sometimes felt all right enough to give a little opinion or slag off the hospital food. I wanted him to understand that I was not this 'person' really, that I was actually quite nice and once upon a time I was actually human. I wanted desperately to be seen as curable and intelligent and not a panic-stricken idiot who would suddenly freeze in morbid terror as an attack crept over her. That was not me, see. Hello!

At any given opportunity I tried to find out from the nurses if they had met other patients like me, with the same symptoms, and were they better now? Were they cured? Did they feel like they could not breathe? Were dying? Were crazy? I guess after a while I sounded like a stuck record because I was told to relax and do something – coloring was always an option or how about weaving a mat? Mmm . . . Yum.

Journal entry: Have had a particularly bad day, I feel like two metal hands are gripping my shoulders and my chest and my bosom area are sore and painful. I have been having awful spasmy, veiny, achey painful pulls in my upper left breast area ... My diaphragm feels swollen and sore ... too scared to sleep, anticipated the worst. Felt disorientated, scared, agitated. Sometimes I want to curl up where no one can find me. I have a pain in my back and front. The undercurrent of miserableness is present. I feel absolutely shitty. I get so angry sometimes when I read all these 'self-help' books and their airy-fairy remedies. It gives me the impression that anxiety and depression are not being seen as an 'illness'. It's like saying 'right now don't take cough mixture, try eating two flowers and stretching'. It's like telling someone not to scratch an itch, not to blink, not to walk ... Who wants to look stupid? Nobody. Only when it gets too much and you're on the point of collapsing you 'might' say something.

God? Allah? Hunched up on the balcony I cried and sobbed and begged and pleaded for mercy, for blessings, for something that would help me. Did He have a spare angel? Where were these miracles I had read about? Was I a guinea pig? Hello up there? It's me yet again.

This illness was causing me to live a different life – a life of medicines and healings, a world so different from what I knew and from what was familiar. People were changing towards me, perhaps out of sympathy, out of embarrassment or perhaps out of disgust at what a stupid cow I was being.

Everything had changed. I did not want change. I was Rachael. There was no need to talk in a cottonwool voice around me, or to behave like Mary Poppins. I could still comprehend every single bloody thing. If everything changed then how would I find my way out of this maze, this turmoil of different feelings that were inside me all day long. There had to be a way out. There had to be. But where the hell was it?

Mrs. Shales, my drama teacher at school, gave me some very important advice once. I had just performed very badly at the Cheltenham Arts Festival, and the judge had torn me to pieces with her nasty criticism. I was naturally very reluctant to do my next piece as I was convinced I would fail yet again. I was standing in the draughty corridors of the Cheltenham Town Hall almost in tears when Mrs. Shales came up to me and said 'Rachael, when you fall off your horse, you dust yourself down and then you get right back on!' She meant it too, and she knew that I could do it. She had faith in me. Mustering all the courage I had I went on to do my next piece, in front of the same judge (who looked decidedly fed up at seeing me again and was probably wondering why I was even bothering). But that piece earned me a silver medal! The judge was not such a battleaxe after all – well, at least she recognized pure talent when she saw it.

Coincidentally, the piece I had performed was from *Hamlet* – Ophelia's 'mad scene'. There's food for thought. OK, I am digressing, but the point is that I got back on my horse. Now if only I could find my horse again. Even a bloody donkey would do at this stage.

Journal entry:
They come unbidden, wild horses unridden,
galloping through the plains of my mind,
'Hush', I say 'Hush. Cease this mad rush
but still they persist, cruel and unkind.'

I was beginning to notice that my patterns of fear were rhetorical, they played the same basic song, only sometimes it was light jazz and at other times heavy metal. In short, the feelings were the same but the intensity varied. The more tense and worried I got, the worse they were. I was the vessel. I was carrying them. Fear, it seemed, can go nowhere unaided.

Journal entry: Don't panic! Push your tummy in and out with deep breaths . . . Look at the sky . . . think of a favorite recipe.

hapter Eleven

Is there a witchdoctor in the house?

Journal entry: The whole day seemed really blurry and hazy today. I felt like I was faraway in the land of plod. I also had a palpitation (I think) and it terrified me and my feet went cold.

Panic disorder is characterized by any one or more of the following symptoms:

Breathlessness
Choking
Dizziness
Feeling scared
Sweating
Chest pains
Feeling distant
Wanting to run

Feeling doom and gloom.
You may even have all of these symptoms in which case
you're really fucked.
(I did, and I guess it shows.)

In Borneo, when you're unwell and acting strangely it usually means only one thing – you have had a spell cast on you. Yes, a spell. In this condition you need to see the *Bomoh*, who is a mixture of a shaman, medicine man and spiritual healer. A Chinese friend of a friend of my mother offered to take me for a consultation. I was too tired to decline and at that stage would have tried anything anyway. My mind was not in. It had gone away, leaving frayed nerves and tense muscles in an empty body. I was so jittery and agitated that I was sure people could hear me rattle as I walked past.

The *Bomoh* lived on the first floor in a block of shop houses in the center of town. Before the appointment we had to buy a bunch of yellow chrysanthemums to be used for part of the ritual. I was starting to feel rather tense, unusual for me. Tense, smothered and about to be 'de-spelled', I followed my Mum and Mrs. Chi up the litter-strewn staircase to Merlin's.

A smiley-faced Chinese man let us in, and as I entered the front door which opened up into a small sitting room the strong musky scent of incense greeted me, and I could just about make out a beautiful altar hung in another room, gleaming red and gold upon which stood a statuette of a very serene-looking Goddess of Mercy. Around the table sat a couple of Chinese men, eating buns and sipping tea. Mrs. Chi said something in Chinese and we were led into the altar room and told to wait for 'the Master'. I wanted to go home. The incense was getting to me and I was starting to feel agitated and yucky. I was in a strange place sitting in a strange place, if you see what I mean. I just wanted out of there.

Eventually, a young Chinese man came in the room, nodded and sat down cross-legged on the floor. Beside him sat his two assistants, the ones who had been scoffing buns earlier on but who now looked very important and wise. Mrs. Chi explained my symptoms to the Master, who nodded knowingly before closing his eyes to contact *his* master, who was from 'another realm' – dead is the popular term, I think.

After five minutes of communication, a diagnosis was revealed. I was under a spell. Someone, although he could not say who, but definitely someone, had taken a dislike to me and that is why I had been feeling strange. Mum and Mrs. Chi listened intently, nodding in all seriousness and looking like what they were hearing was very normal. As for me, speaking as someone who was not feeling very normal at the time it was, as you can imagine, hard to take in. Luckily, though, it was only a weak spell, and could be removed. That was jolly good to know.

Taking into account the time and the effort, not to mention the concern that Mrs. Chi had shown, I duly tried my best to look relieved. 'Phew!' wipe your forehead, big sigh of relief and kudos to the Master for finding out I was under a spell. Nice one! Now, let's get on with the show. Is there anyone else out there who feels they are under a spell? Speak up! Anyone?

One of the assistants told us to sit in the living room while the Master worked on my healing spell. We were given a cup of tea but the buns were finished, so while Mum and Mrs. Chi sat talking in hushed whispers, occasionally looking over at me, I watched telly. After about twenty minutes the Master came out with a list of things I had to buy.

Oh fuck, I thought. Please No. Not shopping. It was an unusual shopping list though – not quite frog's legs and eye of newt but flowers of seven different colors, sea salt and seven nails. That's right, nails. Oh and candles – white candles, which signify purity. Apart from the nails, I could pretty much understand the concept of the spell. It was to cleanse me. The nails were to be hammered into the ground at specific points outside my house, to destroy the negative energies and ensure protection for me.

In this world we meet all kinds of people, but, at the end of the day, as Poppa, my grandad always used to say, 'We must look for the good in everyone.' The fact that these people, who I had only just met, were trying to help me is something I look back on with gratitude. And while I still had a long way to go, the kindness they showed meant a lot to the sulky selfish woman they had to deal with. And maybe their spell did help – maybe the faith and positive energy that they put into it, in a way, eventually reached me. The karmic cycle of life and all.

I had a hell of a job hammering the nails into the hard ground. Our garden at the time had lots of big trees, with long thick roots, and most of the specific points were where these trees were. Plus we had chickens, cats, a sea eagle with a broken wing and a pet goat called Minnie and they were all over the place. Minnie especially kept chewing my shirt as the last nail was very near her enclosure. I lost the whole 'banishing bad spell' mode and nearly hammered her hoof. Then I had my flower bath, and apart from getting a few chrysanthemum petals stuck in my mouth it was very refreshing.

Journal entry:
Some heroes go to battle on bloodied fields,
Some heroes climb mountains, scaling rock with bare hands,
some heroes walk unaided through foreign lands, alone in the wilderness,
Some heroes pace the dark streets at night, seeking out

criminals who lurk in shadowy places,
Some heroes do all of this without even moving,
They simply journey in their mind,
Painfully,
Pathetically,
Poetic justice.
I am turning into an antisocial self piteous cow.

hapter Twelve

Mind over matter

Journal entry: If only the power that my Mind seems to possess could make me feel as good as it does bad. If only I could experience overpowering happiness the way I could experience sadness. Last night was absolutely awful. I felt very chilly and fluey . . . I paced up and down the lounge and hall trying to calm myself, basically it was me trying to tire myself out. Told a lie to Mum and said I would be late because of a meeting . . . in actual fact I felt like shit warmed up in a trance.

I could readily and easily accept the most awful, disastrous morbid scenarios and believe them one hundred percent, but to accept that goodness and wonderfulness and loveliness and joyness existed was impossible. It was all lies. I would look at my family and friends chatting to each other, laughing, washing their cars, cooking dinner, and wonder how they could be so at ease. Were they not worried? Afraid? Didn't they watch the news? How could they even contemplate smiling? Happiness is an illusion, you know. How stupid can you be?

I remember a few weeks after we had moved in to our new house; Mum brought my grandparents round and asked me to give my grandpa a quick tour. I couldn't. It would mean walking and talking and I just froze. How could I possibly take my grandpa around our small three-bedroomed house? Impossible. I just wanted to sit at the table and pretend I wasn't there. The very idea of both walking around and talking made me feel physically sick.

I always understood hell to be a place where sinners would be flung into a burning pit of flames. Naturally the devil in a red dress and horns would be there to poke us and laugh in glee as we (I include myself here) begged for mercy and a drink of water.

But we all have preconceived ideas of heaven and hell. In every religion these places exist and are mentioned both in the Koran and the Bible. And while I'm in no position to dispute religious theory, I'm inclined to say that the mind can take us to hell or heaven in the time it takes to pop a Xanax® in your mouth.

The hell that I felt I was in was gray, full of dead. Dead thoughts, dead feelings, dead trees, dead grass, dead food, dead textures. It was an un-alive place that rejected any notion of a happy existence. I was the same person, but my mind had changed. Was there something more powerful than my mind? What was it? What had programmed my mind to behave this way? Could it be unprogrammed? Where had my mind disappeared to? Had it lost me or had I lost it? Sherlock Holmes would have had a field day – but then again, he was an opium addict so I guess he had his bad moments too.

Throughout this time, my Mum was my rock. She stood by me all the way. I would ring her up at two in the morning demanding to be picked up now before slamming down the phone and hunching over the balcony until her car came. I would snap at her if she asked how I was feeling or did I want a hot drink? I was awful and yet all she did was stand by me.

Day and night, Mum was there to listen to me and to try to understand. I love my Mum. She was totally brilliant. She was there for me throughout and I took a lot of comfort from having her around. Just small things like a hot drink before bedtime or watching telly on her bed. That was what helped me. Just having my mummy around I guess. In fact, my whole family was always there for me. My little men, my two wonderful sisters Jenny and Paula, my grandparents. They never left; every time I disappeared on a journey to my weird place they would still be waiting for me when I got back. As I said, it's pretty powerful, love.

Anyway, after the spell-banishing incident I still was not better. Perhaps it wasn't an immediate cure? Maybe I had to wait until a few full moons had passed? I certainly wasn't feeling any different.

Like I said, Mum was my rock, and she never gave up on me and my mental ailment and was constantly looking for people to help me. This time it was a psychotherapist, an Australian chap who was based at one of the local colleges and who might be able to shed some light on my increasingly darkening world. The fact that he was Australian sounded hopeful. Maybe he would be able to give a different, more laid-back kind of perspective, not as clinical and medical perhaps as the psychiatrists at the hospital. We could throw a few steaks on the barbie, break open a few cans of Fosters and chill out.

I just wanted to be better and I would have done anything. Sad really. As soon as I entered the room I knew it was a mistake. It was the way he was dressed. How can I explain this? It literally screamed expatriate in the orient. Lots of khaki and cotton. When you've lived in the Far East for as long as I have, you instinctively recognize such traits. The whole expatriate 'dress like a colonial' thing. I was expecting Crocodile Dundee and got Dr. Livingstone (I presume). However, we shook hands and I resisted the temptation to say 'g'day mate'. He seemed to be a nice, amicable guy and appeared genuinely interested to find out about my panic attacks. The thing was, as soon as I had sat down and had given him a brief outline of my symptoms I actually felt a panic attack coming on! Right there and then, in front of him!

He obviously had not noticed though, because he was talking and went on and on and on – coping strategies, medications, bla, bla, bla. I wasn't listening, I was tuning out. The leather on the chair was sticking to the back of my hot sweaty legs, my palms were clenched in fear and I was hyperventilating – but I couldn't bring myself to tell him. Not after he had so expertly outlined all the common symptoms and coping strategies: that would have been embarrassing and besides, I had only just met the guy; you don't kiss and tell on the first date. Plus he simply would not stop talking. It was as if he'd swallowed a whole book on 'Coping strategies in nervous anxiety' and was reciting it word for word to me – he'd memorized it and was now being examined.

I had no choice but to practice the only coping strategies I knew: tense up and pretend, dig nails into palms of hands and wait to faint on the floor in a muddled jangled pile of nerves. Painfully try and gasp for breath while being mindful of not attracting too much attention to yourself because, if this geezer finds out you are having a full-blown panic attack he won't know what to do and besides, he is already on the middle chapter about medication and seems well away. While this Sheila was halfway up the billabong tree, waltzing with Matilda.

It seemed to last forever, by which time I was practically glued to the chair in a strange combination of fear and total boredom. Session over I unglued myself, said thank you very much and politely rattled out of the door. He waved me off with a bright smile, obviously thinking he had managed to assist me in some way. I wish he had. Hyperventilating in the car all the way home, once again I felt that awful lost feeling of being unreachable.

Journal entry: I feel like I'm on a rollercoaster. I cannot let go of it, if I let go I will fall to pieces. I am having a panic attack. Either that or I am about to die. I am having trouble breathing. I feel smothered. I feel suffocated. But most of all I feel very scared.

People with nervous illness can come across as very overpowering. All they want to do is talk about themselves and how they have all these symptoms which they are *sure* are serious. They are convinced the doctors know absolutely nothing and they are quite certain that they need specialist treatment. Talking to a person with a nervous illness isn't always easy either – they may fidget, have funny facial expressions, laugh and cry all at once. I never had facial tics but I would sigh a lot and always have my arm slung over my head. I guess I must have looked odd. Very chimpanzee.

Frazzled, that's the word. Frazzled nerves. It's the point where your tightly strung nerves cannot hold you any more and you feel out of control. One by one your nerves seem to twang like overstretched guitar strings and you are left trying to carry on with a broken instrument. It's very uncomfortable being strained and tense and when you start to frazzle your body does all kinds of weird things. Your lips may twitch, your neck may jerk, your eyes blink – because you are starting to unravel. I think I probably used to look like I was break-dancing

Well-meaning folk do tell you to 'Stop jerking your head like that, you look weird', or 'What the hell are you standing like that for? You look like a monkey.' Of course there's no point in saying 'I can't help it', because the enlightened reply will be 'Oh, *of course you can!* Don't be so stupid! Pull yourself together! Snap out of it! Grow up! Be strong!'

If only they knew that simply standing there took a ton of strength and yes, I would love to snap out of it! There is no one more than me who wants to snap out of it! That is why I rarely ventured out. I felt like a freak. Thirty pounds overweight, lank hair and a blank expression, and the monkey pose wasn't exactly enhancing the picture. The only person that I may have been able to have a conversation with during this time was Tarzan.

Like I said though, people with nervous illness want to talk. They want to explain. Yes, it sounds weird and crazy but they want to let it out, and yet a lot of the time they realize that if what they are going through doesn't even make sense to themselves, how the hell could another person understand? Which is why they close up. It's a lot easier to scream into a pillow and scribble into a journal than to tell someone you are being punished by God and a monster is inside you feeding you bad thoughts.

I came to understand that a lot of people do not like to discuss 'those kinds of things'. If it did not fit into the category of normal, like a sore foot or marriage problems, then it was better kept to yourself. Ironically, perhaps one of reasons that so many people do suffer from anxiety and nervous disorders is that they have been brought up to believe that there are some things that you should not talk about or try to solve yourself. Perhaps we have an idealized image of who we should be: not wanting to destroy that image we attempt to muddle through life pretending.

If you cross the line and sound way too weird then you are better being frazzled on your own. That's why it gets so lonely. You are stuck in yourself and no one knows the way out. It has to come from you. I *knew* I was inside somewhere, I *knew* that my thoughts were out of control, I knew this, but where was I going to start? I was aware of how I appeared, that it was a nervous breakdown or whatever, but, still, I had to get out. If I didn't help myself then nobody could. Yes, I was being assisted with psychiatric treatment and had attempted to do the pills, yoga, spells and prayer but still, it was up to me. If it had started in me then it would have to end in me. But where was I to begin?

You see, at the end of the day, no matter how much help I had, I knew and felt that I was alone. But deep deep inside me – without meaning to sound corny – I also knew that I could get better. Even when my head felt like steel and my thoughts were trying to mentally ambush me, I knew. Thoughts are just thoughts for God's sake! You can control them.

I had a strong feeling that the whole of the medical profession in Brunei knew me by now. They probably had a poster of me stuck in their surgeries with a warning sign pasted on the bottom. 'Watch out for this one, multitude of symptoms but is never convinced. Approach with caution.'

Nevertheless it was in my own best interest to get as many second opinions as possible. I mean, what if they might have overlooked something? It was in this frame of mind that I convinced my doctor to book me for a stress test and an echocardiogram. Just to be reassured. To be convinced. Either way, I wanted it. I wanted all the tests on the planet. A very nice doctor, Mr. Luqman, did my stress test, which involved being hooked up to a heart monitoring device and walking on a treadmill. I did very well given my fragile state of mind and he told me with a smile that he 'never wanted to see me again'. This was good to know. My heart was functioning, yet it felt so broken.

Journal entry: I feel powerless, worthless, frumpy, pathetic, lost, alone, faithless, stupid, thick, clumsy, scared, fat.

Today was another hell day. I had those awful windy pains that go up to my throat. I was petrified. I lay feeling my pulse and inside I was screaming with fear. I phoned up the Medical center and put on an Australian accent and pretended my husband had an echocardiogram eight months ago and how accurate were they. Just to ease my mind. I still feel like hell tho.

I snap when I feel scared. Maybe that's what crocodiles do too.

hapter Thirteen

Where are you God?

Journal entry: So, what other alternatives do I have?
My brain is overtaxed . . . mental mountaineering. There
are no words to describe the utter fear I am feeling now.
Doom. My left arm feels tight and sore . . . my pulse is
80 and I am just on edge now waiting. I am scared and
nervous.

Unrelentless. That was the word for my state of mind, but while I battled and fidgeted my way around I was still determined to get better. I was getting angry and in between the attacks and the phobias and the obsessions I was aware that some part of me was still able to think and function. Flipping through the pages of a British women's magazine I happened across an article about a panic support group in England. There was a phone number and you could call at any time of the day or night.

This was just what I needed! Dialing the number I waited for the saviors in England to answer. I was a phone call away from a cure.

''Ello' a rather tired, distant-sounding voice answered.

'Yes, hello . . . I am calling about your advert.'

''Ello . . . 'ello?'

Obviously I needed to speak louder.

'Yes, I am calling from Brunei and . . .'

'Where? Can yer speak up a bit please?'

'Sorry, yes, I am calling from Brunei and it's about panic attacks and . . . '

'Oh roight . . . Broonie? . . . Yer what?'

'It's Brunei . . . it's near Singapore, I said it's near Singapore . . . and anyway it's about the panic attacks and . . . '

'OK, well, there's nobody 'ere at the moment.'

'Ohhh . . . so what should I do because I have panic attacks and . . .'

'Well if you leave us yer address we'll send you a pamphlet o'roight? Cos it's a Sunday see and none of the others are 'ere on Sunday.'

Resigned to my fate I gave the man my address in Brunei and resisted the urge to accuse him of false advertising. I had wasted over three pounds on a two minute call and was none the wiser. However, I will give them credit, within a few weeks I did receive information about panic attacks. The only trouble was, England was too far away for me to attend the weekly support groups.

Journal entry: If God is for me then who can be against me?

I believe in God. The highest power, The Divine. There has to be something responsible for our presence in this world. For you, and for me. So, where was He now? Where? I needed to know the answers. I was scared. I wanted comfort and love and cozy feelings, not this! Not deathly fears and a banging heart, not pains and tension and strange gloomy feelings that shadowed me wherever I went. Even a saint could not put up with this, surely even a saint had a good day? Was I up for a sainthood perhaps? Like I said, the mind plays silly tricks on us.

Prayer became an option; I was raised as a Muslim. A very simple religion whose basic message is 'surrender to the will of God', or surrender in peace, the 'slam' part of Islam has its roots in the word 'salaam' . . . peace. Well, I wanted peace more than anyone, so I duly got out my prayer mat and prayed.

The Muslim prayer involves certain recitations which should be memorized, very simple verses which acknowledge God as being our one Creator. The thing is, I had forgotten the verses. Verses which I had learnt in school, verses I knew! I had to get out a little prayer book and the pages kept flicking over by themselves and my prayer gown was all over the place. It was very distracting and not a special moment at all. The more I tried to remember the verses, the more I would forget. Plus my prayer gown was long and I had to keep yanking at it. I was just so wrong. Everything was wrong and I was a sinner. However, I carried on, and at the end, kneeling on my mat when it was time for my *doa* or personal prayer to God, I fell apart. My body, wracked with fear and tension and the pain of being trapped in this silly stupid mind just shook with sobs and stifled groans of a very sad little girl trying to be a grown-up and failing miserably. Tears gushed down my face and I cried until my eyes were swollen. In this state of mind I lay down on the prayer mat and eventually fell asleep.

Journal entry:
The Lord God who hath made us all,
The tiny mouse,

The mighty man,
He made us and sealed us with His faith,
It's all part of a bigger plan.
So when you falter
When you fall
And when your day seems dark as night,
Reach deep inside
And stand up tall,
For Faith will lead you to your light.

Chapter Fourteen

Prescriptions, prescriptions, prescriptions!

Journal entry: So, what (if anything) helps you in a freak out panic situation? I feel it coming and I tense up ... I try to distract myself ... Went to a meeting ... Felt uncomfortable and my chest felt tight and I had occasional pain. I surged up into panic mode, my feet and hands went cold and I couldn't concentrate, all I kept thinking was 'I'm going to die. . . . I'm going to die.' I had to escape so I made an excuse about going to the airport. Left in blur. Fear, agitation on a scale of 200%. Raced home. Phoned Mum ... broke down.

Dr. Jadish had gone on leave so my next appointment was with a female psychiatrist, who for legal purposes I cannot name here, so let's call her Grumpy Face. I knew I was on to a bad thing the moment I walked into her dim little cave – er, room. She looked over and then briefly nodded for me to sit down. Scanning my notes she informed me that she was 'Putting you on BuSpar®, you can go and get it from the Pharmacy.' That was it? No 'How are you? Anything you want to talk about?' It was intimidating. That's what it was. Bloody intimidating. She made me feel like a complete moron.

I desperately wanted to ask what BuSpar® was, but decided against it and feeling totally stupid I crawled out. She could stick her Buspam or whatever the hell it was called up her bony bottom. How dare she treat me like that? I was a person.

Was that how everyone saw me? As some stupid incapable idiot that could be spoken at and not conversed with? Just shove me some pills and tell me to basically stop wasting her time? Was that who I had become? Someone to be hushed up? To be medicated into oblivion regardless of what my feelings were? Of course I was mad. She was a psychiatrist with a problem and, as far as I was concerned, totally in the wrong profession. She would have been better shoveling compost. That's the polite term for shit.

Note: BuSpar®, pronounced: Byoo-spar

Side-effects: Dizziness. . .

Less common side-effects: Anger, hostility. (Obviously Grumpy Face was on them.)

Where was Mr. Jadish? Had he left because of me? Was he coming back? He was cool. Later that week I got a call from the hospital informing me that as Mr. Jadish was on long leave I had been assigned another psychiatrist, Mr. Keer. My next appointment was in two weeks time. Probably to see if the old BuSpar has kicked, in I thought.

I am not anti-medication. I take Panadol® for a headache and flu meds and antibiotics for a nasty bug. But antidepressants were a different story. Yes, I was aware that there might not be any side-effects, I knew the basic theories and I had considered them all very carefully, but my theories were stronger. I felt that I could not possibly even risk side-effects, what I was experiencing was scary enough, and if my mind and body could create these sensations on its own, imagine what it could do with the aid of an antidepressant? Plus, I had not totally lost my faculties and my ability to think. Yes, it was somewhat distorted and at times defied logic but I was still functioning. I was not a lost cause.

There was nobody who wanted to feel better more than me, but I wanted it to be a natural better. I was also aware that after a year, if you are doing well you get weaned off the antidepressants. In short, it was not a permanent lasting cure, it was not with you forever. What if you relapsed? What if psychologically you once again descended back into your depressed abyss of a mind? And what about withdrawal symptoms? There were no answers because every one of us is different.

Medicine can only give some reassurance but not an absolute guarantee. True, we are very fortunate to be living in a time when good medication is available, I do not dispute that for one second, and I personally have met people for whom antidepressants have made life much better. But in my case, and it is only a little case I know, I did not want to become dependent on a solution that was not permanent, and I knew that my tired mind was in such a strange place that it would probably create side-effects. Such is the power of the human mind. I would sometimes nibble on the corner of a Xanax®, a tiny crumb, just to make me feel better or before bedtime, but it wasn't often and I just kept them for reassurance.

I wasn't being brave, I was playing it safe. Perhaps I let people down, perhaps I hindered a speedy recovery, but I just wanted to get better in my own way, in my own time and somewhere, very, very far away inside me I could.

One method that was starting to help me was 'self-talking'. If a nasty feeling came on heralding a panic attack I would begin to talk to myself a kind of baby language talk. Please don't laugh – well, all right then, do. But it helped. The feelings would start, pounding heart, tight chest, clammy hands, dry mouth, the whole adrenaline spiel and I would talk to myself in a little whisper – 'Right, here we go. You are OK; not nice I know, good girl . . . it's just your fight or flight thingy, keep calm, you know this feeling' and so it went, on and on. Sometimes I would count or write myself through it . . . basically it was the 'good' me taking on the 'bad' me. Now that would give the psychiatrists something to talk about – subject suffering from multiple personality disorder.

I just wanted the answer! The key. I was prepared to try anything and had done. I was seeking a cure, a remedy, a peace of mind. I felt so weak and scared inside. I needed so much attention and love, but had no idea how to communicate with the real world. I was caught up in a spidery cobweb of illusions and no one could get to me.

Journal entry:
Hello anxiety my old friend, you've come to be with me again,
come to haunt me, come to make me mad
come to taunt me, make me feel so sad,
come to laugh as I fall
try to break down your wall
in the search for silence.
(Sung to the Sound of Silence)
Not one day goes by without the beast awakening in a deep, dark crevice in my mind; if only I could reach it I would kill it.

I needed a sign from God. A sign that I was going to recover. After all, He was responsible for this affliction surely? Standing on the balcony at 2.00 a.m. one dark night I looked at the sky. That's where God lives. I was sobbing and my pajama top was wet. With my crew-cut hairstyle and snotty nose I must have looked delightful – baggy saggy body in baggy saggy pajamas.

But I was going to get an answer! I wanted a sign from my Creator. 'Please give me a sign God, show me I will get better!' I cried. 'Please God, help me, show me!' Well, it could have been pure coincidence but at that precise moment a huge star erupted in the night sky, a sparkling display of fireworks just for me. Rooted to the spot I wondered if anyone else had seen it? Bit scary that. 'That will teach you to go asking for Heavenly signs,' I told myself as I scurried in, clutching my pajama bottoms and locking the door. I reckon it was Him though. God was listening. He couldn't afford not to really. I was not going down without a fight.

Journal entry:
I see a door
Slightly ajar
At the end of this road
Too far, too far . . .

Chapter Fifteen

A fellow pilgrim

Journal entry: Sat in office unable to relax. Stared out
   of window. Had a banging heart.
There is no fight without a war,
There are no wars without mankind
But yours is the hardest war of all
It is war of another kind.
But let not go,
Hold on to life
For you belong as others do,
Reach out for love
Reach far and wide
And you'll see what I say is true.
God is love
And we are of He
There is no greater mystery

Yet one thing that is pure and true
Is your love for God
And His for You.

It had been over a year now and I was still trying to work myself through it. Around this time I met a lady whom I will call Seraphin, a fellow pilgrim on the journey of mental enlightenment. Seraphin and I were very similar, both in our thirties with a family and a career. In fact, Seraphin had a very comfortable lifestyle. Her husband had a good job and they had just built their own house. She frequently traveled and seemed to have it all. Isn't that what life is all about? Money and luxuries? No, it isn't. Seraphin spent every single day worried about her impending stroke. She had all the symptoms, she told me, her eyes flickering and her face twitching. Like me, she was convinced that the doctors had missed something and it was up to her to find it and prove them wrong.

Sitting and talking to her was like looking into a mirror. Only she seemed worse. Talking at full speed and tensed up, she looked pale and exhausted. I really wanted to talk about my symptoms too but I could not get a single word in – this was her moment, her time to talk. I sat and listened, selfishly reassured that I was not the only one and realizing at last that there are people who are actually suffering more.

While there might be the same underlying symptoms of breath-lessness, shaking, sweating and nausea in a panic attack, the fears can be very different. In Seraphin's case she was convinced it was a stroke because her one side would freeze and go numb. Others may fear a brain tumor or a heart attack. Some people do not know what they are afraid of and they just need to get away. A panic attack can mimic all kinds of illnesses. They're very clever.

I knew by then that the tingling and numbness sensations was caused by my adrenaline-rich blood, zapping through my body and then leaving me to deal with the consequences. I saw it as a giant head rush, but in this case it was a body rush. The tingling was a giant pins and needles sensation, unpleasant but harmless.

Seraphin was on medication, and she had also sought treatment in England. She was still convinced, however, that it was a physical illness and not a psychological one. Perhaps it was this conviction that was hindering her recovery – perhaps it was easier to accept. Nobody wants to be thought of as mental or crazy. Society is still not too cool about this kind of thing. In my case, however, I was beginning to understand that my mind was out of control and I had to start taking responsibility for it. I had been living in a gray hell and I wanted to move out.

Journal entry: If I were to relax I would have to confront a painful body. The bosom whacks and the pickled onion claw. The Soreioitis in my middle and spasms in my chest. Today I made myself go on despite some fear and discomfort.

Another little sign from God came my way around this time. We were getting quite close, me and God. My aunty who lived in Seattle sent me a little book which had first been published in the 1960s. It was written in a very simple, 'easy for a tired mind to digest' way. It spoke to me, it understood me and it made sense. It showed me that I was not the only one . I devoured it. Every time I felt an attack coming on I would reach for my little book. That book and my teddy bear were my best friends.

I felt a bit hopeful. Hopeful was good. Hopeful signified possibilities.

Journal entry:
I am always somewhere else, in a dark haunted place,
That continuously challenges me.

I fear however, I may becoming a boring victim as the dark-
ness is becoming 'common',
An educated guess would label this 'depression' yet I would
label it 'suppression'
It's a 'dis- ease' of the mind.
Smile and the world smiles with you, panic and you're on
your own.

Knowing I was going to be asked about my medication I was
rather nervous about seeing the new psychiatrist. Would he be as
nasty as the last grumpy BuSpar? one? He wasn't. Mr. Keer was a
very friendly, quietly spoken, bald Nepalese man. Very tidy office
too. I reckon he must have been a Virgo. Well, either that or an
obsessive–compulsive.

'And how are we doing?' he smiled at me from across his big long
desk.

What was with the 'we' thing? It's always worrying when people
speak like that. Was I supposed to answer '*We* are fine although *we*
have had some bad attacks recently haven't we?' But I smiled back,
'All right, bit up and down.'

'That's perfectly normal,' he smiled knowingly. I smiled back too.
He nodded, still smiling. We were having a Smileathon.

'Now then Rachael . . . how have you been with the . . .'

Oh fuckety fuck fuck. The million dollar question was on its way.
The question that I dreaded. Should I say 'pass?' He was staring at
me intently, and still smiling. Fuck. Hoot. 'Ummmm . . . Go on
Rachael! Wipe the smile off his face! He's bald anyway so he can't
tear his hair out. Mr. Jadish has probably told him all about you anyway! He knows you lie about medicine Rachael! He *knows*! He's a
psychiatrist and they are very clever bunnies.

'Ermmm . . . mm . . .'

'I see,' said Mr. Keer in his gentle Nepalese accent. 'You haven't been taking them is it?'

Shouldn't that have been 'we' haven't been taking them? Then at least I could have shared the blame. 'Well, a bit,' I burbled. 'A bit' sounds better than 'Not at all, don't be ridiculous, I spit on the very idea' (preferably said in a very heavy Russian accent).

I went on to explain my fears and my logic and he listened. He really seemed like a good guy and appeared to totally understand where I was coming from. He recommend therefore that I stop the medication for the time being (not that I had been on it) and that I take the mild anti-anxiety pill Activan® if I had trouble sleeping.

The other recommendation was that I 'write myself a letter'. A letter describing my feelings and my emotions, anything I wanted to say to myself and how I thought I could get better. He also said not to over-analyze everything as it would not be useful, and not to read so many medical books. Good advice that.

Later that evening I wrote myself a 'Dear Rachael' letter. It felt odd at first, me writing to me. However when I had finished it was eight pages long and talked about things I had forgotten. My school days, my hurts, my expectations . . . it was a funny, sad letter.

Excerpts from the Rachael letter:

The key to untangling any mess is to slowly unravel it and to untie any knots that you come across. It may take time and patience but eventually you will get there. Anyone who perseveres will always get there. You have a lot of things going around in your head . . . sometimes you wonder who you are.

You are a mother, daughter, wife, sister, but you never belong to you. You want to be heard and you think you are all wrong and nobody likes you. You have always been like that. You worry about your weight, your work; you worry all the time about everything. It's a bit silly, you can't do it all . . . You feel unpretty, unwanted and you dwell on it. Like when you were little and you thought there were monsters at the end of the bed and you had to keep asking if it was nearly morning. You have to start being a bit nicer to yourself and to stop wanting to solve everything . . . you feel scared because you have run out of things to worry about . . . You have to be nicer to yourself. Lots of people love you, your little men and your family. You're bossy but that's OK and you are bad at getting up in the mornings. You are quite a good dresser and you used to love make-up and high heels and dancing. So what's happened? You are in there . . . don't be scared. You are good at pretending though. Always have been. You would rather lie than cause a scene. You hate the thought of people disliking you. You're a people pleaser too, can't say no. And you don't believe in your own talents. You can write songs in a minute, poems . . . but you shove everything aside because in your mind they are all just nothing. You want your husband to treat you like a princess, to feel beautiful and sexy. You want to be strong and brave. You hate who you are. You feel trapped and tired and heavy. But nobody knows because you pretend and it comes out wrong. How long do you want to be like this? How long? Forever? You know, you aren't that bad. You can be quite funny too . . . and the boys love your silly stories and the way you play dressing up with them and make up treasure hunts . . . and you are good at cooking and love being in the garden with the cats . . . Come on now, where have you gone? Rachael, you're still in there somewhere. It's time to come out.

Rachael

Chapter Sixteen

A spoonful of sugar

Journal entry: Will I ever get better? I feel resentful at times and wonder where my life is heading because from where I am standing it doesn't look too good.

But you know, it was I guess — time to come out, that is, of the panic attack closet. The reality of life is such that we put things away in a closet because we are scared of facing up to them. Well, I was. But how much can a body take? We are all struggling with deep dark secrets yet you will still find that there are people who can identify with you. We are never alone. There is always a fellow traveler. Thousands in fact. I was becoming aware of this.

I was still very scared of my illness and it was a very, very private thing to me. What would people say? What would people think? Me? Rachael? A nervous breakdown person? A weakling? Seeking attention and feeling sorry for herself — pathetic.

Occasional moments of clarity showed me how boring this illness was becoming. Yes, boring is an apt description. I mean it would get me all wound up and scared and on edge and yet lead nowhere. It was a fungus. It thrived on my dark, damp thoughts and was feeding off thin air. Weightless and yet poisonous. Like a mushroom. They should rename it 'mushroomitis'.

All my fears had not come true and I was giving these worries more time than they deserved. I *believed* them to be real when in fact they weren't. By hiding our thoughts and worries inside us we think that they will go away, but until you deal with them you will find that they are still vying for your attention, and until they get it they ain't going nowhere. I had become a different person under the influence of this mental illness. I had conformed to its demands. Well, perhaps it was about time it started conforming to mine. 'Hey you, yeah you, ya big fat mushroom, bout time you got your boring little butt outta here . . . this town ain't big enough for the two of us.'

My limitations stopped me from speaking up. They cornered me and said 'Rachael baby, just shut up and get on with it, nobody has time for a moaning Minnie . . . everyone has problems Rach . . . so you got no money, no support and are not too happy in your marriage. Well, Jeez . . . deal with it. Take responsibility . . . be adult! Life is not easy and, except for Christmas and birthdays it is certainly not meant to be enjoyed! The fact you're so miserable proves you are alive! Be grateful you have food on your table and a roof over your head! Grow up, shut up and face facts!'

But then there is another little voice inside that constantly whispers 'Something here's not right and you know it.'

Our body cannot speak to us and therefore it gives us signs, physical signs. When we are stressed our neck may go stiff or we will get a pounding headache, when we are worried we may feel like crying or running away. We may feel like that but we rarely do it. We think that if we struggle on things will get better. We see it as weak to give in to our feelings when in fact it is much weaker to pretend and carry on. All these are signs that we need to listen to. It's not stupid or cowardly to take control of your emotions. It's not dramatic or weak. It's the strongest bravest thing a human being can do and by far the most honest. Be honest to yourself or you will just suffer needlessly. Look what happened to Pinocchio . . .

My mind and body, however, struggling to deal with this conflict of emotions, decided to stick up for me. That's when the panic settled in. The panic was a true demonstration of how I was really feeling inside. I don't want to sound like a know it all, far from it. I know nothing but what I experienced, really. But I do know the awful, struggling, yucky feelings of depression. In fact there are no feelings as such. It's all just nothing. It's because I know that awful dull feeling that I realize we need to start being more honest with ourselves. Besides, I don't think a long wooden nose would make me look too hot.

I was starting to venture out more. My journals would update me on how much progress was being made and if certain days were better than others. My little book would help me read through a panic attack. The gray was still there though. The looming, heavy death feeling. Like an industrial park was sitting in my head. Or like I was stuck in a silent movie full of dead people. To describe that feeling I can only say, it comes before you have time to register. It comes on before you have time to stop it – the awful overwhelming gloom just feeds off you and lets no happy thought in. I had a choice though: to let it overwhelm me or to not let it overwhelm me. There is always a choice, no matter how small, and it was *still* there. At times like this, feeling pitiful and weak, I would get out a favorite childhood book, one with happy stories. Enid Blyton was good and so was Milly Molly Mandy.

Well, it was simple happy reading and there was no pressure. Or, I would watch the TNT channel which had lovely old-fashioned movies; James Stewart and Cary Grant were favorites. Anything that was happy. Even if I could not feel it, I would surround myself with it and hope that it would sink into me. I would light berry-scented candles and watch *Sleepless in Seattle* or color pictures with the boys. Just very, very small things that I could sense and that gave me a feeling of coziness and warmth.

Plus I knew by then that *the mind can only think one thought at any given time*, so by focusing on these little good thoughts, the bad thoughts would not come in. They do say that good overcomes evil. I also had read that hyperventilating or over-breathing could be helped by breathing into a paper bag, thus the genius in me made sure I had a little stock of paper bags. In my handbag, in the car, in my good old bedside drawer. Just knowing I had them around made me feel safer. Plastic bags did not work quite as well. I was not short of breath, I had too much breath. That was all. That was all it was.

So, in a roundabout, somewhat obscure way, I was attempting with some success to crawl out of the abyss so aptly described by Goethe.

Journal entry:
Who am I?
I am you.
I thought I was the only one,
I am.
But there are two.
There's me
and there's me.
But that can't be right.
Its Curiouser and Curiouser.

A very strange sight
There's me in the mirror
and me standing here,
The me that is strong
The me full of fear
The me that is wrong
The me that is right
The me that gives up
The me that holds tight
Then there's I that just wants at the end of the day to
find peace of mind.
Make the insanity go away!
There is something seriously wrong with my left leg. It has
been aching and hurting since last night . . . I don't know
what it could be . . . I was thinking about things I like today
. . . books . . . Snow . . . Still have flu, feel like poo. My leg
hurts. I feel alienated and scared. I feel religionless.

My little book encouraged me to sail through a panic attack. Not to tense up and to contort your body into tight, tense knots of muscle, which only made it worse. I was hardly aware of how much effort it took to go through a panic attack, how much thought and energy goes into creating those sensations. We tense up rigid, then our adrenaline starts to flow, our heart pumps, nostrils flare, eyes widen, breathing increases, sweat pours, mouth goes dry and we stand still, afraid to move. Or, we decide that we need to find a safe place to hide and run off into the darkness.

But what are we afraid of? What is the root cause of all this fear? Yes it may be genetic, yes it may be a chemical imbalance, yes it may be a cornucopia of delights but why do we give it so much power? What exactly can it do to us? Apart from making us feel like there is no hope and we are doomed, it can actually do nothing. Nothing.

It can make us feel like that, the same way as being in love can make you feel like you have butterflies in your tummy, but ain't no butterflies come flying out of your mouth. The same way you feel you could melt when some sexy person looks at you, but – and probably just as well really, it could be very embarrassing – you don't.

Our body is an expert on feelings and our mind fools us into believing them. I began to try and open up more. If I felt an attack coming on I would say 'Oh dear, I feel breathless again . . . oh no.' Only to close family though. Not to someone I did not know. I mean, I didn't sidle up to some stranger in a dark alleyway and breathlessly pant, 'I can't breathe baby, I am so out of breath . . .'

I wanted to be normal but had been fighting so hard that I failed to see the answer was within me. I had been all over the place in my quest for a quick cure, but still had not dealt with my inner feelings – the ones I'd been experiencing before the anxiety came on. The ones about being overweight and overburdened, about being hopeless and that I would never amount to anything. The problems I had been having in my marriage, the daily chores and the worrying about work.

In other words, what had brought this on? What was a panic attack? What causes a breakdown? While I was not able to pinpoint any one thing, I realized that I was being given a wake-up call by Mother Nature. In fact by that time it was Mother Nature, Father Nature and the three kids plus Granny and Grandpa Nature as well. My mind was so full of thoughts that it could not make any logical sense out of them and could only churn out long-forgotten fears. My body, believing these subconscious fears and worries to be real things, prepared me to deal with them by demonstrating physical symptoms. Instead of focusing on what was causing these nasty thoughts I would focus on the pains and the aches, the hyperventilating and the fear. I was blocking out my thoughts and hiding behind the symptoms instead. I was going around in circles until I slowly began to realize that the feelings of fear were just that. Feelings. I would sweat and tremble through an attack, I would lie in fear checking my pulse, I would live in a state of tense, pent-up fear, day in, day out, which never amounted to anything.

I was an ignorant victim. I guess that is why they call it a breakdown. If a car has worn-out tyres, no petrol and a wonky steering wheel, it's going to break down sooner or later. So there comes a point when you have to say 'enough already! I cannot cope and will someone please show me what to do. I have been pretending for far too long and I have things that have worried me since I was a toddler. I need to get it all out. All of it. Yes! I know I am overweight and my bosoms defy gravity! Yes, I know I am not good at math! Yes, I know I get jealous easily! Yes, I know I am selfish!' Let it all out. Shake your gravity-defying bosoms with pride. They are one of a kind.

The best piece of advice I ever read was 'forgive yourself'. That is not always easy. We beat ourselves up with guilt and remorse, but it serves very little purpose. We have to let go sometimes because packing up your troubles in an old kitbag and trailing it along with you wherever you go is impractical. Especially if you have a lot of bags. Then it will be charged as excess baggage and you have to pay more.

Sitting on the balcony one day, I noticed for the first time in two years that trees were green. There they were, in the distance, beautiful green trees. This was such an overwhelming experience for me that I cried. Maybe it was a breakthrough. A breakthrough from my breakdown.

Journal entry: Today when I felt panic and tense and anxious I just carried on . . . There is no way of escaping your thoughts . . . Perhaps one could 'deflect' them though.

hapter Seventeen

The cow looks at the moon

Journal entry:
Bring in the clowns; lets have a laugh,
Bring in the rubber ducky, let's have a bath.
Hallelujah, Hallelujah
So pitifully I sigh
Seated behind my wooden brow,
I am a living lie.
(I reckon I am a closet poet.)

It was now two years and one month according to my journals of scrawls, diagrams, medical terms and poems. I realized that I had come a long way. I was no longer visiting the day ward and had said goodbye to my friends there – people I had come to like and respect. They had a difficult time in that ward and I admired them. Oh, and the staff as well.

Those days that I spent in that psychiatric unit were a real eye-opener. I met people who were lost. I had conversations with people who did not even recognize me the next day. I saw them being taken off for a quick jab of numbness. They would sit there simply staring into space. It hurt me. I felt really bad. I knew that my illness was caused by stress, I knew that. But them? Where were they? The smartly dressed Chinese lady who spoke about home? The pleasant-faced Malay man who would fall asleep in his chair? They were there somewhere, among the old magazines and the clean shiny floors and the hospital smell . . . they were there behind the big locked door and the quiet, stainless steel mealtimes. They were there. Hidden away. Visited occasionally by embarrassed family members who were most probably praying for the day when everything would be all right.

My family were embarrassed. Heck, they were delivering me to a psychiatric ward on a daily basis. Little did they know how much comfort I got from being among these 'real' people, the ones who had decided that this world was not for them and had created their own. The ones who were in so much pain. I defend them all. To the naked eye a person with a mental illness may appear funny and weird, crazy. But if you look at the world from their perspective you will perhaps realize that they are the most courageous people on this earth.

They may be an embarrassment to the conformists of this world, they may say the wrong thing. They may giggle like children: in fact they may view the world from a child-like perspective, but they are still human. And perhaps the reality of who they are, the reality of a mental illness is what scares us. They taught me a lot though. They showed me I was not as ill as I thought. They showed me it was OK to sit and color pictures . . . the world would not stop.

They showed me how lucky I was to not have to endure painful injections and bucketfuls of pills even though they had to, and yet they were still managing to smile at me. Non-judgmental smiles. I felt safe there. I felt OK. I felt that I should be stronger. I felt almost honored to be let in to their world. I was in a ward with patients suffering from schizophrenia, drug addiction, grandiose delusions . . . a place full of 'mental' people. Hell, I have met more mental people in the 'normal' world than I did in that ward. I saw beautiful drawings, weavings and crafts, I saw quiet, polite men and women who would occasionally cry out or talk to themselves. I could only listen. Sitting on my distant chair, trying to draw a picture or read a magazine, I would take it all in. I was not strong enough to help them. I was given a glimpse of something that I will never be able to define, but I respect it. And every day at five, the doors would open and I would go home. They didn't, couldn't . . . perhaps didn't want to and perhaps, deep down inside them they knew that they could never really be accepted. I accepted them. Fuck they were cool. Didn't care what they said or did. They were just trying to live their lives in whatever manner had been made available to them.

I did not like what I saw as far as medication was concerned. Along the way I gradually learnt that a lot of psychiatric illnesses are treated with pills or jabs. I guess that's one way to shut you up. It's basically a huge farce. Medication serves a purpose in that it allows the patient to escape for a while – a brief respite perhaps, disguised in a little capsule saying 'Eat me. Eat me.' Very Alice in Wonderland, and look what she went through.

In short, medication takes us to a different world. I know this to be true. I took pills. They totally disorientated me. My fears and struggles, my worries and fears were still all there but in a far away place. The medication did not work for me. It may have numbed the pain but it did not get rid of it. It was like being drunk. Every time I tried to reach the pain, I would be carried away. The very thing I should have been doing which was confronting my illness was denied. I was taken for a ride.

I remember one occasion when having taken my pills I was out driving with my sons and I nearly overturned on the curb. I felt like a giant marshmallow as I tried to control my car. It was a very mind-numbing experience and as I bumped off the sidewalk and floated around in my little car it was as if I was oblivious to the severity of the situation. That kind of sums up my life really.

I guess along the way, among the fears and weed-like thoughts something happened to me. Perhaps I was beginning to realize that I was able to get through it. That my thoughts could not physically harm me, nor could they manifest and become real. Perhaps I realized that they were epitomizing 'me'. That they were screaming at me to wake up. Only it wasn't a scream, it was more a dull thud. But where did I start? There was no direction – no book entitled 'How to get out of a panic attack and get rid of depressive thoughts forever and be better forever and ever!'

What I didn't realize was that just by being able to go through them I had already made a start. We are always under pressure to get better, aren't we? To be normal and talk about mundane things. But you know, there is no definition of normal, we just have to find a niche and snuggle into it. So many people depend on you. There are so many things you have to do. So many commitments. So much to get through. The list is endless. You really have to hold on to your beliefs, no matter how silly they may seem. And you know, there won't exactly be a day when you suddenly get 'better', there won't be a parade, a big band or fireworks signifying the beginning of getting better, no, there will just be times, seconds, days when you will find you are managing, or perhaps you won't even notice. You can't force getting better.

I called them my moments. And these moments started to get longer. They were moments of clarity, moments of 'hey, I feel OK today', moments of 'to hell with what people think'. These were good moments and when you get them they need to be relished like an egg salad with lots of salad cream . . . or apple pie and loads of custard. But I digress.

I tell you, my 'moments' were what helped me along. I figured that even though everyone was busy talking about me and waiting for me to get better my little moments were what helped me the most. The moment when I cooked a meal without panicking, the moment when I had a whole conversation without wanting to run away, the moment when I sang a nursery rhyme with my little preschoolers, the moment when I felt OK to go for a walk on my own. Small victories but huge milestones.

Please, please, nurture these moments because they are the key to your recovery. They are showing you that you can be all right. They are showing you that you are still capable of getting better, they are reminding you.

Whatever you feel like doing, go for it and sod the rest of the world. If baking a whole batch of muffins, drawing a picture, singing in the shower, scratching your bum or just lazing about can make you feel good and contented then please go for it. That's what cognitive behavioral therapy is all about. No, not about scratching your bum, but it wants to help you reprogramme yourself, retune your behavior pattern . . . it wants to help you seek out *you*, and once you have found you . . . don't let go. (Group hug now please.)

You can put as many fancy names as you want to on the various treatments available for people with a nervous illness, but I know that my little moments, the times that I felt cozy and snuggle-uppy and OK had a bigger influence on me than all the treatments in the world. They were coming from me. The *real* me. Isn't that beautiful? But it's so very true. I could identify with my moments. A picture was forming. I knew when I was happy. I knew what made me content. I could not find it in a hospital or in a pill or in a treatment.

These treatments can't come home with you, can't really fully understand what you are going through, can't hold your hand or cuddle you when you feel like you are about to die . . . but what they can do is give you a guideline, a place to start and perhaps an understanding that you really are not alone.

I wish I had support groups available to me when I was going through my panic attacks. Just someone who understood. Someone to exchange notes with . . . I know it would have helped me. As it was I just had the psychiatric unit available. But there was no way I wanted to become dependent on pills. It was not natural, it was not real and it was certainly not me and while I occasionally nibbled on the corners of a 0.25 mg of Xanax®, it was very few and far between and I eventually lost my little packet.

I decided to do something that would have been totally unheard of two years ago. To open a playschool of my own. Go into business, enter the corporate world. Thus, I opened up The Honey Tree School in a tiny little three-roomed bungalow, not far from my house. With just eight children and one staff member, it was a very happy little playschool. Some days were difficult but overall I was enjoying my little business. Maybe I was too busy to think about being afraid?

I was beginning to drive more now and had even ventured out on the bus with the boys. We went all the way to the fish market before I felt a bit funny and we got back on another bus and went home again. The attacks were not as frequent and they were getting shorter. I was also managing with my self-talk and by underplaying the sensations. They were just silly feelings after all and I had felt them before, yes, they would come but they would also go. If I fainted? Then I would have to be revived. If I felt scared? Then I would have to be scared for a little while but then they would stop.

I also decided to start going for walks. Just little walks in a jungle reserve called Shahbandar Hill. A beautiful natural rainforest, teeming with birds and butterflies and little honey bears that never come out. There are trails you can follow and I decided to try the hill walk. Ha, ha, ha. My sister Jenny zooms up all the hills in the reserve but I decided to opt for the first one. A steep little number that did not seem to have a peak. Like a really bad panic attack I guess.

One day I put on my tracksuit bottoms and sneakers and decided to go for it. I stood at the door and informed my husband that I was off to climb Shahbandar Hill. Me, the plump, nervous wreck of a woman with a big bottom and saggy bosoms, the proverbial cow. I was going to climb one of the steepest hills in Brunei so bite my bum and call me a banana.

My husband, used to me by now, waved me off (probably hoping I would fall over the edge). When I arrived there I stood and looked up at one of the highest hills in Brunei. What the hoot was I thinking? I felt totally odd. All around me super-duper slender people with Walkmans and not a flabby arm in sight sped by. I was not perturbed. I was Mercury, I was faster than the speed of light, I was in control, I was raring to go.

I was knackered by the time I had gotten a few steps up.

After a few more attempts I was beginning to feel rather shaky and scared. I trundled to my car. I shook all the way home and hid in my bedroom. I had relapsed. Maybe I was just unfit. I would try again. Oh yes, I would return.

Journal entry: Life is a series of hill walks. You stumble, trip, and walk. Eventually you become accustomed to the stumbling and learn how to avoid tripping. There is always a hill top waiting to be reached. Today was generally tense ... although I rode it out. I believe that we owe it to who we

are to carry on and to be true to who we are meant to be
. . . no matter how shitty the circumstances . . . it's just an
illusion to better things.

No, I was not suddenly better overnight. It was still around, the fear and the feelings. But having had them for two years they were getting boring and tiresome. Perhaps somewhere during this period I had begun to get better. I had never fully given in to it and even on the shittiest days when I could barely hold my toothbrush to brush my teeth I would keep going. I built up an immunity to it!

I would feel awful for days but I knew deep within me that it would get better; I just had to allow it to happen. I had to stop focusing on it so much. After all what could it do to me? Sure I felt lousy and awful and scared but these feelings could not physically harm me. Yes, they were unpleasant and put me on edge but that was about it.

There were no support groups, no helplines, no counselors, no books, no nothing. For me it was very much a help yourself kind of illness. Help yourself because only you know what you are feeling. Help yourself because you want to get well. Help yourself because nobody else can. Yes, I had my psychiatrist visits, but they were only half-hourly sessions and sometimes I had to wait a couple of months for the next appointment.

Yet again, I got on my tracksuit bottoms and headed for the Shah-bandar Hill. I took it very slowly, stopping when I felt tired and just generally trying to enjoy the view. I wanted to get to the top of the hill, I wanted to have a tight bum like the little show off who had just whizzed past me. Halfway up, I began to feel very out of breath. Was it from the exercise or was it an attack? Oh fuck. I was too close to the top to turn around now. I decided it was just me being unfit, and after a few minutes resumed my uphill challenge.

A panic attack and an uphill walk are very similar: you puff and wheeze, your heart pounds away merrily, you sweat and your mouth gets dry, you feel dizzy and light-headed. It is. What I like to call 'mental mountaineering', very much so.

So, if you are halfway up a hill and feeling all these sensations you would not simply charge off down again pushing other climbers off, nor would you stand there. You would simply rest, let the feelings subside and then carry on. Which is what I told myself as I paused for breath admiring the scenic view of the Borneo jungle. Actually, I hunched up and stared at my muddy shoes, and waited for the feelings to go away.

It's the normal effects of physical exertion. To think of all the hills I had been climbing for the past two years! After one-and-a-half hours, sweating buckets and as muddy as a hippo, I made it. My feet were sore and my face sticky and sweaty. But I was there. It felt so damn good. Me! A panic attack person, me, who a year ago could barely leave the house. Me! It was amazing. The cow had jumped over the moon! Lassie had come home! and somewhere over the rainbow skies were blue!

The other climbers had no idea what a small victory I was celebrating. They all looked pretty hot and bothered so it was not a good time to ask for a group hug. My tracksuit was sticking to my bum so I decided to go home.

Journal entry: Today I climbed Shahbandar hill . . . will do it again next year.

(hapter Eighteen

The cow jumps over the moon

Journal entry: It's possible, anything is possible, and the whole world is not unreachable. Our Soul is Ever-ready to fly.

I want to tell you something. I am not a really brave person. The point is that I did not like being the way I was. It meant having to go through some wretched, terrible experiences on a daily basis. It meant that daily life was something incomprehensible and far away.

Whatever the reasons, the background, the history, the theories behind it all, the one thing I wanted to do was to get better. I wanted it to happen immediately, but like anything that is broken, we first have to get all the pieces and then we start putting it back together again. That doesn't mean to say that we can't make a start.

Getting better is not difficult. Accepting and believing you can get better is usually the first hurdle — you simply do not think that you will ever be free from the anxiety and panic. Getting better is impossible as far as you are concerned.

If you start telling yourself that you can actually recover, there will come a time when you believe it. As you read this you may be thinking 'Not me! She has no idea just how bad I feel! I will never get better!' But I do though, because I felt like that; I lived in fear and I let it take over. My own fears, my own thoughts took over like old weeds and I let it happen because at that time I was too mentally tired to even think rationally. I wanted the quick cures, the magic recipe and the instant betters and I fought too hard to find them. The desperation to get better was very strong and when I could not find cures I felt worse.

We can do little things on a daily basis. Perhaps one of the best things to do is to stop fearing the attacks, let them do their thing and I assure you they will then go away. They are coming from you. You are making them happen. It's so strange to think like that, but it truly is you. The more you fear them the worse they feel. Try distracting yourself, just once, count your fingers, focus on your breathing, talk to yourself, distract your mind from concentrating so hard on your fears. Even when you feel that you cannot fully relax, just tell yourself 'It's only a panic attack and it's coming from me, it will go away in a minute. I know it will because it always does.'

You feel like you cannot do anything and are powerless. You are only powerless because all your effort and concentration is going into that panic attack. Your mind cannot focus on two things at once, remember, so it is doing the best it can to give you a really good panic attack.

I also discovered that I had to find methods that suited me. Methods that I could understand and did not seem far-fetched. I kept it simple. If you have your own methods and they are giving you comfort and making you feel better then use them. My main methods and what I like to term my coping strategies were:

1. Self-talking myself through them and living in the moments of good more than the bad.
2. Feeling my pulse and finding it was not beating nearly as fast as I thought. (70 beats per minute and sometimes up to 80 . . . sometimes even faster!)
3. Letting them come and not fighting too hard.
4. Writing my feelings down as I experienced them, this was especially good for comparing good and bad and shitty days. It also played an important part in making me realize that the attacks were usually similar.
5. Telling myself that I was not suffocating, I was over-breathing and it would subside and that I could always get a paper bag from somewhere!
6. If it came on in a public place then I would excuse myself and go to the loo. It was easier than trying to explain to people. However, if I had no choice I would simply say 'feel a bit tired, carry on, I'm OK'. Minimum fuss.
7. Talking to the psychiatrist helped. I especially found the letter writing useful, and I realized that my anxiety had begun very quietly a long time ago and was now just playing at full volume.
8. A bad day is only that. It does not mean you are a lost cause. Everyone has them. I used to get a bad week!

If any new sensations arise, it does not mean it has gotten worse, it simply means that you are desensitized to the other sensations. Subconsciously you are always scanning your body and actually bringing these new feelings into play.

All those weird spasms, pains, clenches, are just your muscles. They have been kept so tense and stiff from all your fear and worry, perhaps from the way you have been holding yourself, afraid you are going to break. So when you start to unwind they twang in relief – which causes you to worry more! So you start all over again. Your thoughts are doing a mental marathon. If you clench up your fists really hard, as hard as you can and hold them like that for one minute and then release them, you will feel the blood rushing into your palms. Your fingers will ache and feel sore as you unclench them. That's what is happening to your body but on a bigger scale.

Palpitations do not signify a heart disorder, but because you are so alert to your body and all its strange signals you become conscious of how fast your heart is beating. Of course they are unpleasant but they are very common in anxiety sufferers.

You have to give yourself time to get better. You cannot expect it to happen overnight. That is unrealistic. You can begin to work towards it though. It is not a physical illness but a psychological one that manifests itself in physical symptoms.

You may think that the doctor or counselor or support groups don't understand you or that other people are not suffering as much as you are. But people do understand that you need assistance and support. You may want to try medication or you may want to try a natural remedy. The key point is that you want to try. If one method does not work then be assured that there are lots of other methods that will.

The pattern of your behavior goes a long way in deciding what kind of treatment will suit you – I hammered nails into the ground for God's sake.

I used to scream at my Mum 'I can't breathe, I can't, I can't,' and she would say, as would my grandma, 'Well, you are breathing' And so are you. You are breathing – over-breathing and you are going to get better. And you are going to have people helping you all the way.

Journal entry: Hello darkness my old friend, you're not welcome here.
Fear makes the pain worse.
A flower droopeth in the summer sun
Before the day had ever begun
It bowed its head, against the Wind and Wilted
Weak and full of Woe.
Poor flower, Dear flower
Why do you die?
I have no faith,
The flower sigh.
And better I die
Than live in Vain
Its petals trembled
With frail pain.
Thus walked I towards the sun,
And left the flower to face its fate
And when I saw that Shining beam, I
realized that it's ne'er too late.

    I apologize if I have at any point in this book come across as selfish, pathetic, moody, snappy, scared, sad, self-piteous, annoying, agitating, morbid or nasty. I was not well when I kept my journals. I was that person and more. I brought them out to show you what anxiety did to me. To prove to you that it is not nice and it stirs up all kinds of feelings and can make people dislike you. I wanted you to know also that I love my family and friends but during that time I was so lost and tired that all I could think about was myself. It was not selfish; it was me trying to hold on to my sanity. I would frequently wake up my husband or mother and make them pay attention as I was having a panic attack and they had to comfort me!

Then, when it was over, unaware of the pain that they were going through I would once again return to my little world of weird thoughts. My world looked strange to them. I would go from being all right to downright snappy within seconds – they could barely keep up with my mood swings. It was all fear-based.

I want you to know that you are a good person, that it is OK to be scared. It is normal to be at a loss for words or to think you are the only person in the world with such terrible thoughts. You see everything as bad and you fear each day. That is what I went through.

Once I started to get better I carried on going. My school got bigger, I began composing and writing scripts again. I lost over 28 kilos, dyed my hair a variety of different colors, and began to take an interest in myself. I owed it to myself, you do too. You owe it to yourself.

If you can see it as an illness, if you can understand that it is temporary and you are tired and in need of a rest, then you will be helping yourself towards your recovery. Visualize a good day and believe in it. Start now. Your mind needs very little prompting. Once it knows you want to get well it will begin to work with you. Tell yourself that you are going to start getting better.

Even if these words don't make much sense to you at this moment, even if you think you are not strong enough to cope, please listen to me – you can. If you are strong enough to tolerate those awful scary thoughts every single day then you are very much capable of beginning to face them.

Do not try to do more than you feel able. Do not get angry with yourself. Talk to your doctor or counselor, talk to God as well. But don't go asking for signs! There are signs everywhere. Life is going on around you, babies are being born and you are a part of it. No, I am not getting corny; I am reassuring you that your life will go on and get better. At this point you need reassurance. You know, I needed reassurance a lot of times but I rarely found it because not many people could understand what I was going through. Where does one start? How can someone reassure a person who is in so much mental pain that they are barely recognizable? What do you say to them and will they even listen?

Our fears manifest in symptoms, in pains, in physical fears because we have never truly confronted them and yet our body wants them out. That's why the body is pretty groovy, it is trying to tell us that we need to look at what it is we are scared of instead of running away in fright. It's all right though, you cannot help the fears but you can help yourself recognize that the basis of all these fears is somewhere inside you and, not impossible to solve.

You are very brave you know, and you must understand that this is something that will not last, it may not seem like it at this moment but I promise you that if you allow yourself time and if you tell yourself that it's your own thoughts and feelings and that they will come and go until one day they are gone for good, if you allow yourself to start believing this and to understand it's simply your tired mind, then slowly you will start to get better.

If you were not so tired and wound up they would not bother you and you could deal with those spasms and twinges, the tight band around your head and the aches and pains in your body. But you can't. It's like you and your mind are separate entities and your mind is out to get you. A headache will send you rushing out to the hospital convinced you have a brain tumor, chest pains are heart attacks, pins and needles in your arm are definitely a stroke. There is no in-between. You exhaust yourself with worries and your stomach constantly churns with fear and apprehension. You cannot see beyond the pain. You cannot see a happy life, you don't deserve it, you are worthless and your world is hopeless.

Bet you're not though. I bet that you are a very good person, perhaps you are too good. Perhaps you have been trying too hard?

Perhaps you had little self-confidence to begin with? Maybe there have been things worrying you which you chose to push aside? Well, there is no time like the present. To get better. To actually start being a little bit brave and to understand that you are quite simply all pooped out. Start from this point. Just admitting to yourself that you have an illness which is affecting your mental well-being is a good start.

By just saying aloud 'I am pooped out, I am worn out, I have been kidding myself, I have been real worried about . . . I have been pretending to be OK . . . .'

Whatever comes to mind put it on your 'pooped out' list. It won't take a second. If you don't even feel like writing then just say it to yourself. Pooped out and panicky. Pissed off and panicky . . . pickled and panicky. Just give it a name. Identify it. See, you can't start to get better unless you understand that you have an illness which will only benefit from slowing down, and giving yourself enough time to listen to what your mind is saying, and to realize what your needs are.

There is nothing at all wrong with that. Take it from me. You can argue that you cannot possibly have time out, insisting that you're a full-time Mum with toddlers plus a part-time job and a ratty husband to deal with, or maybe you are a jet-setting businessman with deals to make and contracts to sign, you're a teacher, a gardener, a waitress, a security guard, a shopkeeper, a bartender, a doctor, a lawyer, a tinker, a tailor . . . In short, you have far too many responsibilities to even contemplate taking time out and getting better.

One day, when you start to feel stronger you will be able to see that you have a choice in this illness. You can choose to fight, tense up, run around and be frightened or you can choose to say 'I recognize this feeling, I had it yesterday. This breathlessness and fear . . . it's not very nice but it will go away.' The choice is to let them scare you or not. Even if you start to face them a little bit, even just by going through a panic attack you are making tiny yet crucial decisions to start getting better. Your subconscious mind has started to create little patterns of behavior which are going to help you recover. You are making little headways into restructuring your reactions towards panic attacks.

When you are better you will realize how far you have come. You will realize that you have been keeping a lot of feelings inside. You will realize how much your subconscious mind has meticulously recorded your thoughts and fears, some of which have never surfaced until now.

When you are better you will understand that you cannot solve everything, that yes you have made mistakes, but that you should forgive yourself and should move on now.

When you are better you will realize that you are not perfect and that you still love yourself and your family and friends love you too.

When you are better you will realize that certain events triggered off the anxiety and panic, certain feelings that you never quite dealt with and your mind simply got overloaded, and that is why they are stressing you out, as it were. All those feelings, pains, spasms are your thoughts coming out as physical symptoms.

When you are better you will be so much stronger and wiser. You will know not to let yourself go there again. You will, really.

When you are better, think of a little cow in Brunei who regularly jumps over the moon and is happy again. Then you go jump over the moon too.

I look forward to that day as much as you do. I will be with you all the way.

You have only one life to live . . . live it to the fullest! Go on! Jump over the moon!

It's been nice talking to you.

Rachael Malai Ali